W[illegible] Thunder

Whirling Thunder: One Man's Journey Through Native America
By Paul and Harriett Bullock

Published by Piscataqua Press
An imprint of RiverRun Bookstore
142 Fleet St. | Portsmouth, NH | 03801

www.riverrunbookstore.com
www.piscataquapress.com

ISBN: 978-1-939739-62-9

Printed in the United States of America

Photos on 142, 144, 247 by Jack Szelka

www.wanderingbull.com
www.thelittlebull.com

Contents

Whirling Thunder

One Man's Journey Through Native America

? place 221
[illegible] 225
Song 214
" Ind / 292
Winona 102 (page 124)
6 Nations – 105
A [illegible] 106
Whippoorwill Wildcat 111
? Necia 126, Big Tree, Slow Turtle 126, 140, 142
AIS 126
[illegible] music – 126-7
Wildcat 139
[illegible] – 140
On time [illegible] 159

The Evolution of
New England Powwows
1940-2014

Paul Bullock and

Tall Oak 161

Harriett Bullock

Shenandoah 161-2
Running Deer ? 165

FOREWORD

For half a century Paul Bullock and his family have been committed to raising awareness about the Native people of New England. Paul, known as *Whirling Thunder,* grew up in Bristol, Rhode Island and is of part Wampanoag ancestry. He came into the powwow scene as a boy in the 1940s, performing from the time he was 11 years old. By the late 1960s, when he and his six children had become the Paul Bullock family dancers, teaching dances and songs to others, they had made a decision that they would emphasize Eastern dance steps and etiquette at New England powwows. They sought out Eastern Native people as instructors in dance, etiquette and regalia. At a time when the pervasive "Plains look" remained popular in the East, Paul worked patiently to raise consciousness about southern New England Native traditions.

In addition to active participation at powwows, Paul founded a company, The Wandering Bull, to market craft supplies, books, music and regalia both at the powwows, in a trading post in Attleboro, Massachusetts, and through on-line web sites. In the face of strong Pan-Indian influences, he tried to change perceptions through the example of his own family's dress, and by making available the materials and patterns for others to create Eastern-style regalia. Eventually, The Wandering Bull became the largest retail outlet for Native craft supplies in New England.

One of my lasting memories of Paul occurred at a powwow given by the Native students of Brown University. The small Native student group wished to make their presence more visible on campus by sponsoring an annual powwow, to which all Native organizations and dancers of the region were invited. I was seated in the audience, when the head student dancer invited me down to be one of the honorees in an honor dance. I was very nervous, not sure of exactly what was expected of me, until Paul danced by me and dipped his fan to me in acknowledgement, and from then on I felt as if I was in the right place. Paul had that wonderful capacity to understand and utilize the etiquette of the dance, and to show others how to use it. His innate courtesy and that of Native cultural traditions merged into one. He was a dedicated, purposeful individual whose influence during the long, dry period of the mid-twentieth century, before federal recognition of Eastern tribes, helped reinforce the sense of self of Native New Englanders.

Barbara A. Hail
Curator Emerita, Haffenreffer Museum of Anthropology, Brown University

INTRODUCTION

This labor of love started in 2001 when Ms. Meg Worthing of York Beach, Maine approached Paul requesting his help with a project for her Culture, Tradition and Diversity course at the University of Southern Maine where she was studying in a Master's program. Since this sparked a long held interest, Paul enthusiastically accepted her request.

In part, the Foreword in the original transcription was as follows:

"This is just the beginning!!! As you all know I'm the great procrastinator. For years I've been talking about writing a book about the evolution of Indian Powwows in New England during my lifetime. My entire family has offered to record, transcribe, or word process my endeavors and I have neglected to follow through.

"This abbreviated venture comes about through the kindness and strong encouragement of Ms. Meg Worthing of York Beach, Maine who asked me to talk about my life story as part of a course at the University of Southern Maine, Culture, Tradition and Diversity.

"We spent a number of hours with the tape recorder – she transcribed it for me and sent the copy to me (on the internet!!). Harriett and I corrected the time sequence and attempted to correct memory lapses, etc....

"Meg has suggested using this as a basis and adding

additional 'chapters'...

"Some of the future writings will elaborate on stories already covered and some other things will be covered as well."

From that time on we worked on the future "chapters" – some times more diligently than others but we enjoyed the "reliving" of some of the happiest times of our lives. Unfortunately completion was still in the future when The Creator came to take Paul on his next journey on February 18, 2014.

With the help of my family, I have attempted to complete what had been started although we know that there were many more details that only Paul would remember and many more people who had an impact on the culture and on Paul. Completing this work has been my privilege and my pleasure - any omissions or inaccuracies, although unintended, are mine.

It is our hope that the reader will enjoy this and learn something about the Native culture and the importance of Powwows in New England.

Harriett Bullock
June 2014

DEDICATION

This book is dedicated to all those who have listened intently at a Powwow, or danced their hearts out in the circle, who have labored long and hard over a craft project or item of regalia, who have sung the old traditional songs, who have spent time researching a project, who have been respectful and kind to others, who have listened, learned and shared with others. To all those good and kind people we offer our heartfelt gratitude.

It has been our honor and our privilege to see this project to completion. This project, which has been the dream of Whirling Thunder for many years, is meant to enlighten and enrich the lives of others as Native Cultures have enriched ours.

This humble man helped shape and now chronicle the landscape of Powwows in New England and beyond. This is his story - the story of the evolution of Powwows and of his life - a life of honesty, integrity, and tireless pursuit of enlightenment and education.

Anyone of you who have attended a Powwow at which he was Master of Ceremonies can attest to his desire to educate and share Native Culture. He spent considerable time over the years doing school programs for it is the children who are the future and it is the children who need to learn and have an appreciation of those around them.

His legacy and his wisdom continue in the lives of those he touched and those he loved.

ACKNOWLEDGMENTS

With grateful appreciation we acknowledge the assistance of Meg Worthing, student, teacher, and friend, without whom this book may never have been written. Meg helped get thoughts organized and words on paper. This dream of Whirling Thunder's may have continued to be just a dream without Meg's encouragement.

Barbara Hail, Curator Emerita, Haffenreffer Museum of Anthropology, played a valuable role - guiding and encouraging along the way. Her knowledge of the Culture and interest in the project were instrumental in keeping the wheels turning.

Jack Szelka, "photographer extraordinaire," has shared some of his photographs which have been his life's work.

We appreciate the opportunity to have spent time with Princess Winona while she recounted her life story and the guidance of June Little Winona in verifying the details of her mother's life.

Esther Clear Sky offered guidance with the Star and Clear Sky section and support and encouragement in general. Star had been most helpful in recounting his early years and his time in the service of our country.

Burne Stanley Peters, President, Massachusetts Center for Native American Awareness, willingly verified facts when consulted.

Don Brennan, M.C., Dancer, historian, and friend was always Paul's "go to man" with any questions about various Native Cultures. He always seemed to have the answers.

We appreciate the help and cooperation of Shelah Slade in reviewing the section on Chief Marie Smith Jones.

Additionally we want to thank those of you who have spent countless hours reading and rereading, suggesting revisions or corrections, whose work has smoothed the path to completion.

We are grateful to each of you who have assisted in any way, large or small - we could not have done it without you.

We are also grateful to Tom Holbrook of Piscataqua Press, who has graciously and willingly offered his professional expertise and guided us along the way.

PART ONE

WHIRLING THUNDER'S MEMORIES
TAPED 2001

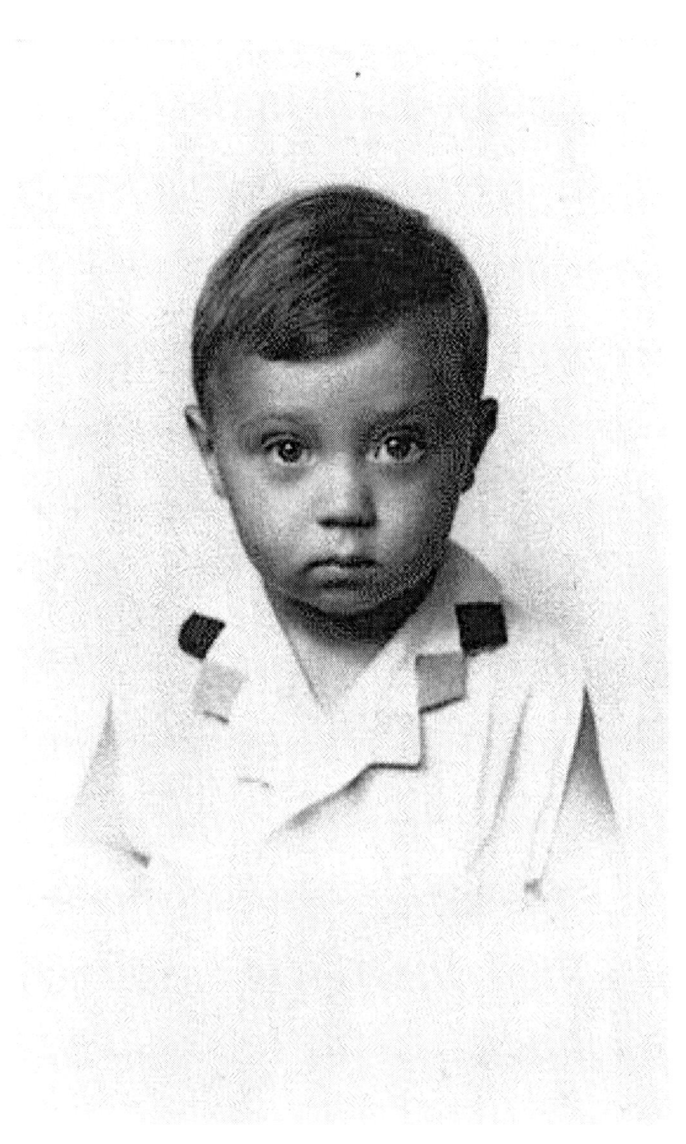

Paul, Mid 1930s

THE EARLY YEARS

I was born in 1931 in Fall River, Massachusetts. Although my parents lived in Bristol, Rhode Island, the most convenient hospital facility was in nearby Fall River. I was told that the hospital was on the trolley line but I am not sure how significant that was in the decision. At that time, many babies were born at home with a midwife or neighbor in attendance, but my mother chose a hospital birth. The family story has always been that it was an extremely long and difficult labor and delivery. My mother and I were in the hospital for two weeks, so things were a little different than they are now.

My mother, Pauline Sylvester Bullock, was born in South Bristol, Maine in 1900 and moved to Bristol, Rhode Island very early on, probably when she was three or four. She didn't really remember living in Maine; she was brought up in Bristol, Rhode Island. I believe that her father, Rosco Sylvester, who was a carpenter, moved to Rhode Island seeking work as a ship builder. He died in the early 1900's and I don't think that my mother remembered him. My maternal grandmother, Martha Gamage Sylvester, raised seven children by herself. They were Clara, Myrtle, Nell, Nan, Charles, Pauline (my mother) and Helen. Another boy, Percy, was drowned in Maine at the age of seventeen, before the family moved to Bristol, Rhode Island. It was very difficult in those days to be a widow raising a large family. In later years, my mother told many stories about their early poverty. Even such things as chocolates were a real luxury to this family. On rare occasions when receiving a chocolate, she would make it last longer by removing the top layer of chocolate and eating the filling with the head of a common pin.

My father, Harry Howard Bullock, Sr., was born on Lafayette St, in Attleboro, Massachusetts in 1897. Lafayette Street is only a few blocks from where I now live. My father had two brothers, Ernest and Edward, and one sister, Evelyn Doris (always called Doris). While in Attleboro, he was a paperboy for the local newspaper. At that time, papers were sold on street corners rather than by home delivery – his corner was in the center of the community at Park Street and Railroad Avenue. He often told us about buying his newspapers for two cents for three newspapers. He in turn, would sell the three papers at one cent each. He would never leave his corner until he had sold all of his papers. One snowy evening, his father, in an effort to get him to come home, bought his final newspaper. This dedication to work and determination to complete the job was evidenced throughout his entire life.

His family moved to Bristol, Rhode Island around 1910 probably because there was work in the textile mills. My grandfather, Henry Bullock, was employed in textiles for the remainder of his working career. I didn't remember a great deal about my grandparents but as I continue this narrative more and more details come to mind. We lived next door to my paternal grandparents, Henry and Emma T. Anderson Bullock, in Bristol when I was about five or six years old.

My grandmother was not well – she suffered from diabetes. She passed away in 1939. It was to this house we always went when we wanted a snack. We'd just go in there and help ourselves to anything that was in the refrigerator, except when the radio program, "David Harum" was on, and my grandmother would listen to that faithfully. When you went into the house and "David Harum" was on, you had to be very quiet and you wouldn't get any conversation. My grandfather worked long after my grandmother died. This household was maintained by my unmarried Aunt Doris, and her unmarried brother, Uncle Eddie. An oft told story was of my grandmother Emma Anderson Bullock throwing her wooden shoes into New York Harbor as the ship upon which she had traveled from Sweden approached the dock. It was felt that she did not want to appear different or strange when entering this new land.

Paternal grandparents, Emma and Henry Bullock, 1938

My father started working when he was fourteen years old. In those days many youngsters had to leave school and go to work. He was an extremely intelligent and very clever person in spite of his limited amount of formal education. He could do most anything he set his mind to and do it well. Bristol was a textile town and my father went to work for a company called Collins & Aikman, and worked for them for forty-two years. In the 1950's the northern textile community suffered from a very poor economy. Many New England textile companies went out of business or moved their operation south in order to take advantage of cheaper labor. Foreign competition, too, became a factor in this economy. After forty-two years of faithful service the company decided that my father "didn't have enough experience," and they let him go. At that time there were no accrued benefits available to those who were dismissed in this fashion. So after all those years of service he had no medical insurance, no vested pension, no life insurance, and of course, no job. There were very few opportunities available for men in their fifties who had spent their entire working years in the textile industry, which had now moved south. Fortunately, my brother Bob, who with his family was living in Connecticut, was able to assist my father in locating a position in a piano factory in eastern Connecticut. My father was a very talented woodworker - this was the ideal opportunity to utilize these talents.

I was the youngest of three boys. My brother, Harry, born in 1921, was ten years older than I, and Bob was 6 years older than I. Because of this age difference, I don't remember much about Harry during my early years. I was the baby and the "brat" in the family and he was the teenager. I'm sure Bob also considered me the runt of the gang.

Paul's parents, Harry and Pauline

Even though those early times were Depression years, I was too young to realize the enormity of the situation. My father always had work and we did not experience the extreme difficulties that many families did. I don't think that my father lost any working time during the Depression although I believe that he had to accept pay cuts during this time. The normal work week was six days and he maintained this schedule until the very late 1930's.

For the most part, Bristol was a textile manufacturing community and most of these companies operated twenty-four hours a day. My father was an overseer. They did not call them foremen or managers at that time – the term was overseer. He supervised about one hundred people (most of them women) and had management responsibilities for all of them during the twenty-four hour work day. His responsibility extended to the employees of all three shifts.

Many families were finding it extremely difficult to make ends meet and people frequently were giving or lending others food, clothing, or money to tide them over the difficult time. My folks were able at one point to purchase a ton of coal for less fortunate friends during one harsh winter. Although my parents considered it a gift, their generosity was repaid albeit after a considerable length of time. These proud New England families did not accept charity easily.

My mother and father enjoyed more than fifty years of married life. Although my father suffered with prostate cancer for fourteen years prior to his death in 1971, my parents had many happy times. They had a wide circle of friends and had many pleasant times between the flair-ups of this disease. They were able to return to Bristol, Rhode Island where they spent the last few years of their lives.

SOUTH BRISTOL, MAINE

In 1937 or '38 my father purchased his first automobile. This new mobility enabled my family to travel to South Bristol, Maine where Mom had been born and to renew acquaintances with many cousins and other family members. South Bristol is located near Damariscotta, just north of Brunswick. It is on the end of one of the many peninsulas in that area. Roads being what they were at that time, it was an eight hour ride which I did not tolerate well. We all enjoyed being in Maine in spite of the long tedious ride to get there.

Heading into the village of South Bristol, Maine

The first couple of summers we camped at the home of Grammy Lou and Lifey (Lucinda and Eliflet Gamage). Lucinda was a first cousin of my grandmother. They had a blueberry patch in their side yard where we pitched our tent. Their home was a big old farmhouse with a barn attached. The outhouse was way out in the rear of the barn. This arrangement made it possible to utilize the facilities in the wintertime without going outside. Grammy Lou was a fastidious housekeeper and painted the privy annually, usually in bright colors. It was also decorated with old calendars with bright pictures, which may have been ten or fifteen years old at that point. It was wide and it was a "three holer" - it included a large, a medium and a little size to accommodate every need. It was always a thrill to use the "three holer."

During our winter visits we would stay in the farmhouse with Grammy Lou and Lifey. Lifey was a retired sea captain and seemed to me to be quite elderly and not very active. He was very friendly and I enjoyed listening to his tales of the sea. They had a cold cellar beneath a trap door in the kitchen floor, where they kept their provisions for the winter. The main source of heat for the entire house was a big wood burning kitchen range. There were registers in the ceiling, which were kept closed during the daytime and opened at night. Big pieces of soapstone were heated on the back of the range, wrapped in flannel and brought up to the bedroom a few minutes before bedtime. Once placed under the covers they warmed the blankets and made bedtime a cozy experience.

A view of our cottages and the water
in South Bristol during the late 1940s

In the late 1930's my parents bought a very small cottage in South Bristol. It was situated on the top of a hill, and had no water supply and a very small plot of land. We would journey up and down the hill to Ted Farrin's well with two buckets – this was our water supply. My parents, over the next few years, added a screened porch, a small kitchen to the south and two additional bedrooms (called bed chambers) on the north side.

They sold that property just after the war ended and bought a large piece of land with an old farmhouse, which was located on the water. They had an artesian well drilled and built a small rustic restaurant in the lower part of the barn. They also built six cabins and my mother operated this business for several years. I spent at least two full summers assisting her. The business, of course, was seasonal and my father remained in Bristol, Rhode Island working at Collins & Aikman while we stayed in Maine. He would drive up to join us weekends and

The Farm House with Paul's barn in the background, South Bristol, Maine, 1947

vacations.

My main function in this enterprise was being the short order cook in Paul's Barn Lunch. Along with the usual hot dogs and hamburgers, the blue plate special was fried mackerel. Tourists would come in and order the mackerel, I'd run out the back door and down the hill to the dock, get fresh mackerel out of the barrel, clean them and bring them back up the hill, roll them in corn meal and cook them. There was always a barrel of fresh fish at the end of the dock. The fisherman would come in all during the day with their catch and replenish the supply of fresh fish. Many of my early memories centered around these experiences in Maine.

Some of the family – Paul, grandmother Martha Sylvester, Lucinda and Eliflet Gamage (Grammy Lou and Lifey) Late 1930s

Harry, Paul, and Pauline Bullock at Paul's Barn, South Bristol, Maine

WORLD WAR II

In 1941, when I was ten years old, World War II broke out and Harry immediately enlisted in the Army Air Corps. He served and trained in a number of locations in the States, and was ultimately stationed in England where he flew many missions over Europe. Bob, who was still in high school, was anxious to join the service, too. In his senior year he tried to enlist in the Navy; however, his age prevented this and my father would not give his permission. Immediately upon graduation, he joined the Navy serving in the Caribbean. At the conclusion of World War II, Bob was in the Pacific Theater on a mine sweeper. They were charged with the job of sweeping mines from the rivers of China following the retreat of the Japanese. I missed my brothers a lot and anxiously awaited their homecoming. To me they were heroes.

With Bristol being right on Narragansett Bay and very close to Newport, Rhode Island there was much Navy presence in our town during the war. I can remember my father bringing a sailor home for dinner on at least one occasion. Perhaps somewhere in the country there were parents grateful that their son was getting a taste of home cooking. This was just another aspect of everyone being involved in the war effort and doing what they could to help out.

The Big Three - Bob, Paul, and Harry in later years

During the war, my father worked very hard; all the factories switched to defense work and his was no exception. My mother, who had always been a "stay at home mom," joined the women of the community to take on defense work in a local factory. She worked at a company which manufactured wire, and she also participated in various support organizations such as the Red Cross. There was a lot of work and the pay was pretty good during the war. The community thrived.

Brother Harry, 1944

Brother Bob, 1944

BOY SCOUTS OF AMERICA & AMERICAN INDIANS

Paul at Scout Camp Yawgoog,
Rockville, RI, mid 1940s

Even though I had spent a considerable amount of my childhood in Maine, I was still a Rhode Islander. I always considered Maine as vacation time and Bristol, Rhode Island was really home. One of my first ambitions was to be old enough to join the Boy Scouts. I remember going down to the parish hall where Troop 5 met, sitting on the fence and looking through the windows at the kids standing awaiting inspection. My friend Beans, who was nine days younger than I was, and I went down to the Scout hall the first Wednesday evening that we were twelve years old. I don't think that we had ever heard of Cub Scouting at that time but Boy Scout Troop 5 was what we wanted to join. This was the epitome of success.

As far back as I can remember, I have always been interested in Indians and Indian Lore and my experiences in Scouting fostered and furthered that interest. In fact, I was active in Scouting until I was twenty one years old and entered the service.

Even before joining the Scouts, I was interested in all things "Indian." My childhood had been filled with stories of Indian ancestors. This made me eager to learn more and membership in the Boy Scouts certainly accelerated this interest. This proved to be a lifelong journey. I spent a lot of time in the woods and a lot of time reading about Indians. At this time there was not a lot of Indian activity in the area, which made it necessary to go further afield. I located names and addresses of some of the old Indian supply businesses (Plume Trading & Sales Co. and Pawnee Bill's Indian Trading Post in Pawnee, Oklahoma) through Scouting publications. I spent my very limited resources to purchase some of the basic supplies needed to get started. From time to time local Indians would come into the community and lecture at various organizations. Small groups also regularly set up their wares and performed at New England Sportsmen Shows. My parents were most cooperative in helping me to attend these events whenever possible.

Miss Jessie Molaske, who was the school librarian, met with us every week for a period of library study. I thought that this was a most boring period. I guess it showed, because finally one time she took me by the collar and asked, "What do you like?" My response was "Indians and boats." So she got me going on some books about Indians. Our friendship intensified over the years and when I was in high school and later, she consulted me regarding new books on Native American subjects, which she was considering purchasing.

Although my Wampanoag heritage is through my father, my mother was very interested in Indians and Indian people, so she and I spent a lot of time studying. Books were expensive and sometimes difficult to locate, but she always purchased Indian books for me for birthdays and Christmas. This was a habit she continued until her death in 1972.

Aunt Doris Bullock who always encouraged Paul

My Aunt Doris also enthusiastically supported this interest. She was a teacher and was frequently able to get new books at discounted prices. Most of these books are still in my possession - a treasured collection.

Meeting Indian people, and particularly local Indian people, was an important part of my life. At this time there were only three annual Powwows in the area. They were primarily family gatherings and had been held for many, many years. The Narragansett Indians held a tribal meeting in southern Rhode Island. The Wampanoag held an annual gathering in Mashpee, Massachusetts and the American Indian Federation, which was an intertribal group, gathered annually at their hall in Lafayette, Rhode Island. The Mashpee people had been gathering for 200 years. This was a long history for this rich culture.

The American Indian Federation Powwow was first held in 1931 and has been held continuously to the present time with very few exceptions. I believe the organization was originally formed by local New England people and evolved into an intertribal group for those who came from outside the area as well. I later had the honor of being Chief of the Federation for approximately seven years - more about that later.

World War II was in progress and gasoline was rationed. My family had an "A" card which allowed us to purchase a very small amount of gasoline – of necessity our travel was much restricted. Whenever possible, my parents drove me to these events.

At this time in my life I was primarily interested in crafts and regalia making and dancing. It wasn't always easy for a youngster to get involved. There wasn't much for a little guy who was probably more interested in the outfits and clothing than these new friends were. I met some people as a youngster, lost track of them for many years and was later able to renew friendships as an adult.

MOUNT HOPE

Bristol is the ancestral home of King Phillip. He was the son of Massasoit, who was the Sachem of the Wampanoag Federation at the time of the landing of the Pilgrims. The Wampanoag village was located on the highest point in town, which was called Mount Hope. In the 1940's these lands, including Mount Hope, were owned by the Rudolph Haffenreffer family. Although it was private property, the public was frequently allowed to enter and view the historic sites. My favorite was King Phillip's Chair, which was a very high rock formation with an indentation in the rock forming a natural chair. I often imagined King Phillip sitting in his chair meeting with his braves, who were sitting on the ground before him with a huge campfire illuminating the entire area. There was a monument in a swamp nearby, which marked the site where King Phillip (Metacomet) had been killed in 1676. There was a cave along the waterfront, which we called Crystal Cave. This was an interesting crystal-like formation which was popular with souvenir hunters. A little further to the south was a huge white rock from which a fresh water spring flowed. I don't know whether the spring and the cave were used by the people in King Phillip's time. I have asked people recently about these two sites and I believe that they may be no longer visible.

Mr. Haffenreffer also owned the Narragansett Brewing Company and was very active in other commercial enterprises. He owned a large farm on the property and hired many people to manage the farm for him. His interest in Native American artifacts led to his lifelong hobby. He accumulated many items from the New England area and over the years his interest expanded to include all Native American groups. This interest led to the formation of the Haffenreffer Museum in a building adjacent to his barn. After many years at this location, the current owner of the museum, Brown University, is in the process of relocating it to Providence, Rhode Island, closer to the campus on the east side of the capital city. (As of the 2014 writing, Brown University has relocated the exhibit area to Manning Hall on the Providence campus. The Bristol site remains a research and collections storage area.)

As a youngster, I remember hearing many stories about his

early collecting endeavors. During the Depression, many local people found artifacts and trinkets in the area and brought them to Mr. Haffenreffer, who would buy them for his museum. These local artifacts, when added to his extensive collection, combined to form one of the largest private Indian collections in the region.

It was a splendid museum, but it was privately owned and public access to it was limited. It was open on occasion to Scout groups, garden clubs, Masonic groups, etc. I was always looking for an excuse to be included. I would go in with the Garden Club, a church group or any other invited organization. Occasionally one of my family members would be included in a group and I would go along with them.

I guess I felt that Mount Hope was my second home and I was over there all the time playing in the woods or along the shore. It was, however, private property and Mr. Haffenreffer would ride in his chauffeur-driven limousine and travel the narrow roads around the estate. On one occasion, Mr. Haffenreffer had the chauffer stop and ask who I was and what I was doing there. I was quite frightened and tried to explain my interest and enthusiasm about Mount Hope. He explained that many people who trespassed over there would do a lot of damage, but said that he had no objection if I went on to the Mount and caused no damage. I met Mr. Haffenreffer a number of times after this through my Scouting experience, but probably spent more time with him in this first meeting than during any subsequent conversations.

One of the men who had been hired as one of the caretakers of the cattle just happened to have a son, Wallace, who was a classmate of mine. His family lived on the Mount in housing supplied for the workers and their families. Wally and I spent a lot of time playing in the huge barns and haylofts. The cattle, which were housed in the barns, all had individual pens which were immaculately clean, and each had a plaque with its name emblazoned on it.

WORK ETHIC

All through my life my father was a good influence and certainly was instrumental in my character development. He taught that it was always possible to do a good job but it was more important to do a little bit more than the job required. Many years later when I was taking a school course in public speaking he advised that good public speaking was easy as long as one knew what he was talking about. He always emphasized being honest, and telling the truth and expected everyone else to do the same.

Most youngsters during this period were paid small amounts for doing chores and running errands for neighbors and friends. I always enjoyed working and had twelve or thirteen regular customers for whom I cut the grass and tended their gardens and lawns. I worked almost all year round for these same people - in the wintertime shoveling snow from their paths and driveways and carrying wood or coal from their cellars into their homes. I earned all of my spending money, paid for Boy Scout camp, and paid for many of my clothes with my earnings.

From the 9th grade through high school, I worked many hours a week after school and weekends at Usher's Farm which was located in the northern part of town. Although I enjoyed this work considerably, I never felt that farming could be a lifelong endeavor for me.

NATIVE PEOPLE

During this time I spent a considerable amount of time also writing letters to Indian people whom I had met through my contacts with Powwow friends and businesses such as Plume Trading & Sales Co. I am sure that I pestered many of them asking questions, trying to get them to write to me and to teach me about Native Culture.

One of the first people I met, a gentleman by the name of Jules One Arrow Hayward, was particularly helpful to me - providing information as well as addresses of different organizations. I am unable to recall his tribal affiliation. He published a newsletter called "Talking Leaves." (Today the newsletter of the American Indianist Society is called, "Talking Leaves".) Mr. Jim Luongo at Plume Trading & Sales Co. was also very helpful and many times over the years I would either get a ride to New York City or hitchhike (which was an acceptable mode of transportation at the time) to the famous 155 Lexington Avenue, New York, New York address. I spent many hours talking with Mr. Luongo

Mr. James Luongo, founder of Plume Trading & Sales Co. in New York City

and his many customers who were coming in and out all day long.

Plume Trading & Sales Co. moved its mail order sales and museum to Munroe, New York in 1957. It was not until 1970 that I visited the "new" location. At that point we went to the store and museum with our six children. Mr. Luongo was there but I don't think that he remembered me from so long ago. This is really not the end of the story as far as Plume Trading & Sales Co. goes. We will pick that up later in this narrative.

Some of my newfound New York friends invited me to participate in a Powwow that was being held at the New Haven Arena in New Haven, Connecticut. I think that I attended this event twice. I remember one year my mother drove me to New Haven and I also remember taking the train from Providence, Rhode Island. I had made a full regalia (perhaps it was less authentic than I intended) but I was quite proud of it and the other participants were most encouraging. Most of the Native people were Iroquois living at the time in the New York City area. There were other tribes represented as well. I remember a gentleman whose name was American Horse and I believe he was Sioux. There were a number of Shinnecock people who came from the far end of Long Island.

Tipis had been constructed on one end of the arena. There were a number of Indian people with horses and a large contingent of re-enactors dressed as early Cavalry soldiers, complete with a canvas covered wagon pulled by horses, which raced around the perimeter of the arena, pursued by the Indians.

I regret that I can't remember more details - I don't remember there being a Master of Ceremonies nor can I remember who provided the music for the little bit of dancing that we did. In retrospect, I believe that this was probably one of the last of the Buffalo Bill type programs that were held throughout the country. We didn't have an Annie Oakley but it was a lot of fun. I am sure that the outfit I had at the time was most amateurish and stereotypical (Western style headdress etc.) but it was comparable in workmanship and style to the outfits worn by the other young people participating. I remember meeting an old man in the changing room and I asked him where I could leave my suitcase and street clothing. "Oh," he said, "leave it right over there. There is not a white man who gets down here today."

I met another "old fellow" at this time. He may have been in his fifties but he seemed very old to me. He was a very tall, distinguished looking man and his name was Harold Davis Emerson, PhD and his Indian name was Be Be Cay Can. He said that he was the last living "Pontiff of the Mayan Temple." He lived in New York City and worked in a professional capacity. It may have been at one of the many universities in that area. We spent a lot of time talking together and later communicating by mail. His early advice was that "An Indian has to be good because you stand out if you're not good. People can do things which are wrong and get away with them, but an Indian doing the same thing will not get away with it." I will always remember him for that bit of advice.

Most of the people I met during this time were from the New York City area. At the time, Brooklyn had the largest concentration of Native Americans on the East Coast. Many of these people living in this area came to the city to work in the high rise construction business. Their real home was Caughnawaga, a Reserve just south of Montreal, Canada. The Mohawk people were adept at working at great heights and

New York offered the best opportunity for this type of work. In many cases the men worked in the city during the week and drove home to be with their families on Friday afternoon, returning late Sunday night to start another work week. Many families lived in the city and maintained a second home at Caughnawaga. This reserve is now called Kahnawake.

Our friend Twin Skies (Louie Deer) was brought up on Caughnawaga and moved to Brooklyn to work as an ironworker. Not all of their work was in New York City, and one of his earliest jobs was on a bridge which connects New London, Connecticut to Mystic, Connecticut. One of his chores was to "get the beer." He would walk across the steel beams to the other side of the river to make a purchase at a local package store. He used to say that if you started off at that job you knew whether or not it would work out because if you made a mistake and fell you lost your job. He married a girl from the reserve and he and Green Leaf (Louise) lived in Brooklyn where they raised their two daughters. As the children were growing up it was not possible to go home to Caughnawaga every weekend as so many of his coworkers did, but they did manage to spend as much time as possible at the reserve. After Louie's passing, Louise gave me permission to name our grandson, Erik, Twin Skies in honor of Louie.

It was only natural that a group of Native American organizations flourished in the New York/ New Jersey area and there were an increasing number of Powwows and public events at that time. As World War II ended in 1945 the Boy Scout program took on new enthusiasm. During the war, those men who could have served as leaders and committeemen were either in the Service or working hard on the civilian war effort - making it very hard for the Scout troops to remain active. Narragansett Council BSA hired Charles (Swede) Harrington. His Indian name was Trail Maker and although he was not Native, he was well qualified to teach Indian lore to the Boy Scouts of Rhode Island because of his long term interest and involvement in Native crafts and culture. He traveled from troop to troop teaching those interested how to dance, construct their outfits and do craft work. He had served in the U.S. Marine Corps. The story goes, and I believe it to be true, that upon receiving his discharge at the end of World War II Swede went into Plume Trading & Sales Co. in New York City and purchased an entire Indian outfit from Jim Luongo. Swede took off his dress blues, dressed himself in his new outfit and traveled home on the bus. The only regret his mother had was that he no longer had his dress blues. Whether or not the story is true is incidental, but it does indicate the amount of interest Swede Harrington brought to the youth of Rhode Island.

BOY SCOUT DANCE TEAM

Swede probably had at least seven or eight boys from each community in the state with whom he worked with the goal of having them all participate as a single unit - the biggest and best Boy Scout Indian Dance Team in the state. This activity enabled me to meet young men throughout the state of Rhode Island so that we could share a common interest. We came together numerous times to put on dance programs around the area. All of this was a part time occupation for Swede. His profession was working with handicapped children at the Gordon School on Providence's East Side.

The Boy Scout program was to culminate in the spring of 1947 at our version of a council wide "powwow" at Mount Hope in Bristol. Unfortunately the selected weekend became famous as the "downpour of the century." The "powwow" and the dance program were never held. Many of the youngsters I met during this program became lifelong friends. Some of them were to re-enter my adult life. Imagine my surprise thirty years later when I learned of a group called The American Indianist Society, which was headquartered in Wilkinsonville, MA. While attending some of their events, I found a number of "Swede's boys" who had maintained their interest and enthusiasm for Native Culture over the last twenty-five years.

Paul in all his Western finery at a Scout dance team event

During this time my interest in all things Indian continued. I was, of course, active in Boy Scouting and so many of the Scout teachings are based on Indian practice that I was able to combine these two interests. I formed a small dance team in my Scout troop. These youngsters made their own outfits and we performed for various youth groups in the Bristol County, Massachusetts area. I always felt that this strengthened their Boy Scout interest and they have all become honorable adults. At least one of them graduated from West Point and one was a graduate of Annapolis.

In 1945 as World War II ended, I was attending high school and became interested in automobiles and discovered girls. Although I was busy with these other endeavors, I was still corresponding with many of the Indian people in the New York area and I attended as many local events as possible. At this time, it was common practice for local Native groups to attend county fairs to perform and sell their wares. I am sure these early contacts included Princess Red Wing, Princess Nashaweena and probably Princess Winona. Although I did not know them well at this time, many years later I was very fortunate to enjoy their friendship. More about this later.

NATIVE IDENTITY

Over the years I tended to give people the impression that it was my mother who fostered this interest. However, my father was proud of his Wampanoag heritage and supported me as well. He was working six days a week and had little time to devote to transporting me; however, my mother was able to do this for me. I remember that he frequently gave me money so that I could order some of the things that I needed. During this time, many Native people did not acknowledge their heritage but I do not think this was the case with my father. We were accepted into the mainstream. There weren't many Indian people in Bristol and it wasn't an issue. When a minority stood out it might have been picked on, but that was not the case in Bristol. In the 30's, 40's, 50's and even into the 60's, many people would not identify themselves as Native.

We met such a woman when my boys were in Boy Scouts in the 1970's. She lived in the Taunton, Massachusetts area and had lived there for a very long time. Her husband was a contractor and she was very active in Cub Scouts. Nobody knew that she was an Indian until her kids went to school and were getting history from the white man's perspective. Unable to tolerate what she considered historical inaccuracies, she announced that she was Native and was going to teach her children history from the Native perspective. She had been brought up not to tell anyone she was an Indian. Even after leaving the Maine, she had maintained this secret.

We were active participants in the American Indian Federation Powwows in Lafayette, Rhode Island at the time. She accepted my invitation to attend the Powwow, however reluctantly. As she stood at the circle and watched the dancing and listened to the songs, she cried. All the cultural things that she had been denying for years, came back to her. There are many people like that. This is very common in the east and to a lesser extent in the West because the Western people are a bit more stereotypical in appearance. They are more identifiable and it is more difficult for them to get into the mainstream.

In the 1980's, people were more willing to come out and identify as Native, but there are still some who have no desire to. They remain in the mainstream. There is divisiveness even within a family. I know of two or three families like this. In one case one brother was very active in Powwows, spiritualism, wore an outfit and was proud to be Native; his brother denied his heritage - had no interest at all in the Native Culture. The brother is now in his seventies and has suddenly become very interested in his culture and genealogy. It is unfortunate this change came about after his brother's death.

Some of the participants at Lafayette Powwow, 1980. Chris and Carolyn Bullock, Faith Bullock, Paul, Louise and Louie Deer, Evelyn Hickman, Ben Massey

FIRST "REAL" JOB & THE DRAFT

In 1950, I started to work in the steel business. The Korean War was just starting and I was still involved with the dance team in Bristol. Crucible Steel was, at the time, one of the largest producers of tool and alloy steel in the country. I was employed in the Providence, Rhode Island branch and the manager was a very nice fellow who happened to be an old Swede. When he learned that my grandmother was Swedish, we had a common bond. He also was very interested in my enthusiasm for everything Indian. He encouraged me to maintain this interest, which I did.

At this time, a number of young men I knew were joining the Service. The draft was in effect and many were being inducted. I had to decide what to do. I could enlist, wait to be drafted, or join a Reserve unit such as the National Guard. There were a variety of deferments as well. A friend of mine who was a World War II veteran and a Marine Reservist, tried to talk me into joining the Marine Reserves, as this would be a way to avoid the draft. If you were in the Reserves, you would serve your duty at home with one or two active duty weekends. I decided I would not do that and very shortly after this decision, the government activated his unit and he was shipped over to Korea immediately. He served there for a long time.

If you enlisted in the Service you were not guaranteed your job upon discharge. If you were drafted, however, your employer was obliged to give you a comparable position upon your return to civilian life. I had a good job and I wanted to stay in the steel business. When my draft number came up sometime in 1951, my company did whatever they had to do to get me deferred from active service because steel was a most critical industry and they needed experienced people. Reluctantly, I took the first deferment. The next time my number came up, in 1952, I requested that the company not attempt any further deferments. I wanted to go in, do it and get it over with. So I was drafted.

I remember the night before I left home, we had a get together with all of the guys. We knew that the Army was inducting a lot of people and we had heard a rumor that the Marines were drafting a few. I didn't mind being drafted and I would go anywhere, I just did not want to be a Marine. The next day at the Induction Center (there were quite a few of us from Bristol who were bused up to Providence) I went through all of the physical exams and was walking down this long corridor where an Army Sergeant with a clipboard waited. He asked, "Your name Bullock?" I replied in the affirmative. He said, "You are a Marine." So I ended up in the Marine Corps. It was the surprise of the century for me.

I had a friend who was a Supply Sergeant in the Army at Fort Devens. Additionally, a friend of my boss was a Colonel, also stationed at Fort Devens. Supply Sergeants swing a lot of weight in whatever branch of Service they are in and Dick was going to nab me when I arrived at Devens. I would have been all set with a choice duty or so I thought. Of course, an Army Colonel also has a lot of authority and would have been able to oversee my training. I had this all set up - in the Army. Of course, I ended up in the Marines. It was an experience I would not change for the world. I think that this was the most broadening experience I have ever had and I am glad that it worked out that way. But I'm sure there were many days in boot camp that I didn't think the Marine Corps was the best place for me.

Paul, 1952 – A proud U.S. Marine

While I was in the Service my parents moved from Bristol to Barrington, Rhode Island, which is about ten miles away. In the whole process of moving, much of the clothing and outfit parts that I had made either got lost or perhaps discarded in error. At any rate, much of it was no longer available to me, with the exception of the books. Additionally, in returning to civilian life and getting involved in a career, my interest certainly wavered for a period of time. I had some very special pieces of beadwork which I had accumulated and these were nowhere to be found. I remember one piece in particular – as a youngster I knew there were differences in beadwork design – basically the Western designs were a lot different than the beadwork produced in the East. The Eastern beadwork is mostly floral with single curves and double curves. Western beadwork, on the other hand, is made up of geometric designs. At that time in my life, I was much more interested in the geometric designs of the west. Many years earlier a junk dealer in Bristol (as part of the war effort the Scouts would collect newspapers, rags and recyclable metals and deliver them to him) called me because he had an item he thought would interest me. It was a women's blouse made of heavy muslin type material with floral beadwork on the sleeves and bodice. It was a beautiful piece of handmade beadwork, which I cut up, mounted on a heavy panel, and used to decorate my Indian shirt. This very special piece was lost to me forever with that move.

ONE FATEFUL EVENING

I was discharged from the Service in 1954 after serving the required two years, returned to my parents' home and resumed work at Crucible Steel. One early June evening, I joined my mother in the side yard. My mother was talking with a young lady and two small red headed children were swinging on our lawn swing. My mother said, "I want you to meet this girl. This is Harriett Mulligan." So we talked a bit and I thought this was a young mother with two children. But I found these were her sisters and she was taking them for a walk. Harriett was indeed a young lady not attached, so I was quite impressed. (I originally narrated this and said that it was spring. Harriett advises that it was the third Monday of June of 1954.)

At this time in my life I had a dog, which had been given to me by a Top Sergeant when I was in the Service. This was a "Marine Dog." He was well trained, smart and great company. He was also very fond of ice cream. In an effort to appear casual and "cool," I put my dog in the car and drove around the corner to Harriett's summer cottage. Fortunately, Harriett liked ice cream and liked my dog, so my casual approach worked. Harriett and I were married two years later.

Paul and Harriett at the beach house,
Barrington, RI, 1954

This change in my life left little time for Indian activities. Although my parents and Aunt Doris continued to tempt me with new books as gifts on special occasions, between starting a family and working, my time was limited. As our children came along we had even less time and money for other interests. I finally reached the point that I knew that I had to become involved. I had to do something and, of course, I had long since committed the address of the Plume Trading & Sales Co. to memory: 155 Lexington Ave, New York "whatever" New York - this was before zip codes. I sent for a catalog. I tried to explain to Harriett what we were going to do, and I really needed to just get in right up to my elbows. Again, the Western influence prevailed. I purchased a kit to make an Indian headdress, a typical Western headpiece. With the kids assembled around the table we started to make the headdress and I just felt that this was a new beginning. Although the children were very enthusiastic, I found that this was really a craft project for adults. So I taught them to carve and paint small Kachina dolls, which I had done in my youth.

We were living in Attleboro and Harriett's father advised that there was an Indian fellow who lived on Holman Street and asked if I knew him. Since I did not know this man my father-in-law urged me to meet him. So one day I hopped in the car, went up to Holman Street and looked him up. His name was Charles Wells and his Indian name was Chief Leading Canoe. He was past Chief of the American Indian Federation. I had known some of the members of this group years ago. The Federation Powwow was coming up and he invited us to attend. This was in 1963 .

GETTING INVOLVED

The American Indian Federation had been formed in 1931, the year I was born. They'd been having an annual Powwow continuously since that time. We brought the three kids and I saw some people I had known before and thoroughly enjoyed the day. Princess Red Wing was in attendance and of course, Princess Nashaweena, Squaw Sachem of this Federation. I am sure that Princess Winona was also there, although I don't remember meeting her that day. We later became members of the American Indian Federation. Princess Winona and Princess Nashaweena became lifelong friends of the family. We also attended many Powwows with Princess Red Wing, who did not belong to the Indian Federation but was most active in Narragansett/Wampanoag Indian activities. This is where the family involvement started.

We became active as a family and as in all intertribal organizations family participation was important. Harriett became very active in a supporting role. Naturally, our children had to have outfits as they learned to dance and they enthusiastically participated in the Federation Powwow for many years. Some of the people whom I had met many years ago attended this Powwow and it seemed as if life had taken a full turn - we were once again involved with the Iroquois people of my youth.

The North American Indian Club in Willimantic, Connecticut was very active in the early 1970's. They, too, put on an annual Powwow, which attracted spectators and dancers from the New England/New York area. We would attend as many of their meetings as possible and spent a lot of time

The kids' first Powwow - Andy, Chief Leading Canoe, Chris, and Betsey at Lafayette, August, 1963

driving to and from the Willimantic area. I served for at least one term as a member of their council.

Occasionally we found ourselves in the position of putting on a Powwow. We were invited at one time to put on a Powwow/program at the Slater Mill complex in Pawtucket, Rhode Island. Slater Mill was the first textile mill in colonial America. In addition, we organized a Powwow at Salve Regina College (now Salve Regina University) in Newport, Rhode Island. We worked frequently with Star and Clear Sky, Pueblo people who were living in Beverly, Massachusetts at that time.

We traveled throughout the state of Massachusetts with them doing programs for the various Deerskin Trading Post locations. We also performed at the Topsfield Fair for several years with Star and Clear Sky and their family.

A favorite summer trip was attending the Indian League of the Americas Inc. Powwow in Barryville, New York. Barryville is located along the Delaware River near the New York/Pennsylvania line. This organization was made up primarily of Mohawk people who lived in New York City and Brooklyn, although their home was a reserve just south of Montreal, Canada. These people were the iron workers who were instrumental in building bridges and skyscrapers in the New York area. The sponsors of this Powwow were the New York Mohawk people, who were joined by their families from Caughnawaga Reserve for the event. This was a very popular intertribal Powwow and the "regulars" represented many different tribes living in the New York/Pennsylvania area. There were Shinnecocks, Lenapes, Sioux, Hopi, Seneca, Navajo, Seminole, Onondaga and Huron to name a few of the many tribes represented. The ironworkers' unions, as well as the owners of the companies, were very supportive of this event and the Powwow attracted numerous busloads of people from the metropolitan area. Vacationers made it an annual event in their summer schedule.

In 1980, we were invited to go to Pointe Bleue, Canada, which is 228 miles north of Montreal. We went with Bright Canoe (Johnny Diabo) and his nephew Albert, from Caughnawaga Reserve. Pointe Bleue is a Montagnais Indian Reserve on Lac Saint Jean. To get there, we drove to Montreal, stayed on the Reserve overnight and drove up to Pointe Bleue the next day. We were to put on programs of Native dancing all week, during their summer festival.

This trip was one of our great family adventures and our children enjoyed meeting all of those people. We found various ways of spanning the language gap - they spoke either French or their native language. Dan, who had two years of high school French, helped us when Albert was not around to translate for us. We will continue this story at a later point in the book.

BIRTH OF THE WANDERING BULL

As the family became more involved in Powwows and similar events, the kids encouraged us to develop a small part time business. All we needed, they advised, was a small card table upon which to place our wares. This would not only give us a headquarters but it would provide Harriett with an opportunity to participate more fully and we suspected that this also provided a place to keep their suitcases and extra regalia during the Powwow. We purchased one dozen boxes of note paper with an Indian design. We sold the first dozen and purchased two dozen. A little later, we made contact with a fellow in Chicago who sold embroidered patches and we purchased inventory from him as well. The boys were corresponding with a number of people who were willing to sell craft supplies to them at wholesale prices. Harriett very early on established a reputation for making ribbon shirts and soon had orders for all she could produce. Of course, these sales enabled us to attend Powwows and pay for gasoline, food, etc. Although everything was informal at the beginning, this was the beginning of the Wandering Bull.

Andy in the early years of The Wandering Bull, 1984

In the early 1970's, our friend Paul Fadden, proprietor of Sam One Bull's Trading Post, was thinking about changing his focus. For some years he had been setting up trade goods at Powwows in the area, but he wanted to liquidate his business and go back to his first love - Powwow dancing. The timing was opportune and we purchased his stock, which gave us a much wider range of offerings. Our fledgling business was underway.

Over time, we increased the number of items we purchased for resale. We found that people in this area wanted and needed craft supplies that were not readily available in New

England. We also found that new mail order companies were springing up all over the country. Earlier, Plume Trading & Sales Co. and Pawnee Bill's had dominated the market for these items.

INTERESTING GROUPS

We also became very friendly with Princess Winona, who is Androscoggin, Wyandot, and Passamaquoddy, originally from the State of Maine. She was then living in Worcester, Massachusetts. We worked very closely with Princess Winona over the years, putting on programs and Powwows and later forming the Indian Cultural Art Lodge. One of the benefits for our children was exposure to this intergenerational group. They met other adults and learned to respect and appreciate older people. They were comfortable with adults and they all became well balanced individuals as a result and developed a great work ethic. True to the Native culture, Elders were revered and respected.

A gentleman who had been a member of the American Indian Federation for years always had a dream of having his own group and a small piece of land. He lived in Plainville, Massachusetts, which isn't very far from my home. His name was Big Thunder (Fred Reynolds). Big Thunder finally took the plunge, got a number of us together and went through whatever legalities were necessary to receive a state charter. This was the formation of an organization called the Wollomonuppoag Indian Council. This group was chartered in 1974 and the organization continues today.

Although we may not be members of all of the following

organizations, we are affiliated with these groups and lend our support: Massachusetts Center for Native American Awareness, The Organization To Preserve Indian Culture (TOPIC), Wollomonuppoag Indian Council, Dighton Intertribal Council, New England Native American Institute, Nipmuc (Chaubunagungamaug Group), Webster Nipmuc Group, Hassanamisco Nipmuc, Greater Lowell Indian Cultural Association (GLICA) and the American Indian Federation. Some of these groups run Powwows periodically; sometimes an organization will run a Powwow for the sole purpose of raising funds to pay organizational operating expenses. Most of the groups support various Native needs and charities such as scholarships, social service programs, health programs, food pantries, public education, jobs, housing, and political action. While Powwows serve purposes, they are basically social in nature and provide us with the opportunity to meet with friends and relatives from the entire area. We look forward to each one because we know that we will meet certain people there who may only attend that particular Powwow. This becomes an opportunity to renew old friendships and get updated on relatives. I will devote more attention to the evolution of Powwows in the New England area in the book.

Caughnawaga Reserve has always been a favorite place for family visits and we will long remember our visits with John and Minnie Diabo and Lou and Louise Deer. One time when the kids were younger, we journeyed to Caughnawaga and stayed with John and Minnie Diabo. The purpose of this trip was to put on a dance program to help raise money for a new furnace for one of their local buildings. Here we were, coming up from Attleboro, Massachusetts to an Indian Reserve in

Canada, to dance because there were not many people on the Reserve who had outfits or were interested in dancing. Times have changed and Caughnawaga (now called Kahnawake) hosts an annual Powwow on the second weekend of July, with thousands of people in attendance to watch three hundred or more dancers.

OUR FAMILY

Our children have grown up, married, pursued their careers and are raising children or have grown children. Their busy schedules preclude them from being as active as they formerly were, but their interest seems to be as enthusiastic as ever. Our youngest daughter, Faith, is called Popshela which means "Wild Flower." When she was given this name by Princess Nashaweena, this was indeed an appropriate name for her. She attends dances whenever she can. When the family first started participating in Powwows she was only about four or five years old. Popshela became a great dancer and won many prizes for her dancing ability. She frequently participated in our school programs when she was growing up and was very much at home at all of the Native events she attended.

Ed was also very young when he began dancing. Princess Nashaweena named him Eyes That Shine. This name was certainly appropriate for him at the time and remains most descriptive to this day. As a youngster, he was primarily interested in Fancy Dancing and frequently participated in school programs with me. As a teenager he had a summer job at the Goldenrod Restaurant in York Beach, Maine. He worked for several seasons and upon graduation from the University of Lowell, he realized his dream of opening a store in York Beach, selling American Indian goods. He had spent a considerable amount of time working at the Wandering Bull in Attleboro and named his new business *the little bull.* His first store was a closet sized room, with no facilities. His business grew rapidly and he relocated to a much larger storefront. His "full time job" keeps him busy as a manufacturer's rep for a number of companies and individuals who produce fine Indian crafts. The *little bull* sells finished products such as moccasins, jewelry and pottery. This is definitely a seasonal store, although the season continues to grow longer each year. He was the lead singer for the former 101 Drum. Ed still manages to attend many events in the Native community.

Dan was named Brown Bear by Princess Nashaweena. He is a great dancer and over the years won his share of contests and participated in many Powwows in New England, New York, New Jersey and as far away as Canada and Alaska. In today's corporate world, he is an engineer with a limited amount of time and a growing family. A singer with the former 101 Drum, he has attended many Native events in the area. His interest tends toward Native textiles and pottery. He has attended Native American antique and craft shows all over the country.

Chris lived in Attleboro until he moved to Washington, New Hampshire where he now operates The Wandering Bull, LLC. He proudly carries the name One Feather, given to him many years ago by a Mohawk Elder. He is well established in both the local community and the Native community. His interest and enthusiasm for Indian arts, crafts, and dance has grown over the years. He also sang with the former 101 Drum. His area of expertise is beadwork (antique and contemporary) and quillwork.

Andy, called Gray Hawk, has always been interested in our Wandering Bull activities. He has been dancing since a very early age and has constructed a number of fine outfits. He is an outstanding craftsperson and has always been willing to share his knowledge with interested people. He went to college at Trent University in Peterborough, Ontario where he majored in Anthropology and Native Studies. This enabled him to develop a wide circle of Canadian Indian friends. After graduation, Andy returned to the States but did not want to go into the corporate world. It was his ambition to expand our business and at the same time provide a better location for our customers.

The family at Aunt Doris's in Bristol, RI

Our eldest daughter, Betsey, was a teenager when we became active at Powwows and as the Wandering Bull business started to grow. She had many friends on the Powwow circuit, attended all of the weekend Powwows and was an enthusiastic camper. She graduated from high school and went to the University of Utah in 1975, later transferring to the University of Chicago, where she completed her studies. She is an accomplished seamstress, and helped out by making ribbon shirts. She also has made lovely finger woven sashes.

OPENING THE STORE

In 1981, a friend of ours had a storefront rental available. Upon inspection we were awed by the "huge" size and concerned with our ability to fill it. Ralph Zito offered to partition the space so that we could have only one half. This would be a major decision for us… I was still working full time in the steel business, Harriett was working full time as a social worker and we still had three children at home. This would be a part time venture for us and Andy would devote his energies full time to the business. In addition to the size of the store, I was concerned about committing to a lease. I asked Ralph how long a lease we would need to commit to. His reply was, "If you come here and you are happy, you will pay the rent. If you are not happy and you don't do well you won't be able to pay the rent. So what good is a lease?" A handshake sealed the deal. Ralph partitioned the space and we moved in.

Prior to the move, the Wandering Bull had been doing business at Powwows and in a portion of our cellar, which was set up as a small showroom. Customers would either purchase from us at Powwows or come to the house by appointment. We still have a number of customers (friends) who reminisce about our little store in the cellar and tell about the many happy evenings spent selecting beads, hair pipe, and craft supplies or chatting over a cup of coffee.

Of course, Harriett is, and always has been, the center of all of our activities. Her reputation as a seamstress continues to grow. She has made Comanche wedding dresses, researched

View of the store from the street

and produced MicMac coats, Indian capotes, and dance shawls, as well as her well-known ribbon shirts.

The new store opened. Andy was the sole employee, chief cook and bottle washer. Ralph, ever the friendly landlord, would stop in frequently to deliver delicious Italian food straight from his kitchen. Andy was always well fed there. It took a while for our customers to find him. He started with a little cash drawer and a sales book in which he recorded each sale.

It is hard to believe but we remained at the same location for twenty four years. Ralph retired a number of years ago, leaving his son, Al, to carry on the tradition of being a friendly and supportive landlord (the meals stopped though.) We did learn that it was a simple matter to fill our "half" store. Over the years we were able to expand our original space to encompass three full store areas plus a large warehouse and storage area. In 1985, we purchased Plume Trading & Sales Co. - the very same Plume which guided me through my youthful interest in all things Indian.

After twenty four years at the Attleboro location, we packed everything up and moved the operation to Carver, Massachusetts. This move was long in coming - Andy lived in Middleboro and Carver was right down the street for him, while it meant a forty five minute drive for Harriett and me. We scaled back our hours and Andy and his wife, Janyte, devoted their energies to running The Wandering Bull in Carver. Although it was primarily a warehouse operation, many customers found their way to our door and enjoyed poking through all of the stock while we pulled and shipped mail orders. It was a good time in Carver but after four years, Andy and Janyte decided to move to Canada to be closer to her

Andy hard at work in the store, 1984

parents who were more in need of their care and attention.

Our dilemma was solved when Chris and Carolyn decided to carry on and relocate the business once again, this time to Washington, New Hampshire where they were living. With renewed vigor and excitement, they will carry this family business into the next decade and beyond, serving our customers at Powwows, via mail order, or even in person for those who brave the dirt road to visit the barn/warehouse on the side of Lovewell Mountain.

Attleboro, Mass.

Carver, Mass. Paul and Harriett

Washington, N.H.

OUR ALASKAN EXPERIENCE

Midnight Sun Intertribal Powwow, Fairbanks, Alaska, July 2001 - Back Row: Dan, Paul, Harriett, Chris Front Row: Michelle and Ed

A friend of ours, Don Standing Bear (Don Forest), has lived in Alaska for over 30 years. He was raised in Massachusetts and comes to New England whenever possible to visit his family. His dream of putting on an intertribal Powwow in Alaska was realized in 2001. He invited me to be Master of Ceremonies and also invited the 101 Drum to participate in this first ever intertribal Powwow in Alaska. This Powwow was also held in 2002 and 2004 and I had the honor of being Master of Ceremonies at all three events.

This was an unforgettable experience. We learned about the state and about its Native population, and we met many wonderful people.

We wore our Eastern clothing and some of the Alaskan people had never seen this type of regalia. It was a learning experience for all of us. Their beadwork is different from ours - we use wampum shells and they were unfamiliar with that craft. They use a lot of moose and caribou for their leather work and moose hair for embroidery and basket making. I will expand more on this later.

Our main objective through the years has been to educate both Indians and non-Indians about Native American Culture. When I was out in the real world working, I would frequently take one of the weeks of my vacation to go to schools to put on programs for the students. All of the family participated whenever possible. In more recent years, Ed and I have been able to do many programs together in the New England area. Our schedules have been more flexible than those of the rest of the family.

I consider myself very fortunate to have had such a wonderful and happy life, a great family, wonderful friends, and many memories and I look forward to documenting more of these happy adventures.

PART TWO

THE CIRCLE OF LIFE

WHIRLING THUNDER (Paul Bullock)
with Harriett Bullock
Written 2002 - 2014

Paul doing the Pipe Ceremony at Limerock Powwow, 1977

"A powwow is a unique experience. To spectators attending for the first time, who have not had the opportunity to mix with and meet people, it is a colorful exhibition of music and dance; to people who regularly attend it is a moving, warm, comfortable experience; and finally to the participants, it can be considered the joy of reunion.

"The word powwow is derived from an eastern woodland Indian language (pau wau) and means medicine man, shaman or healer. Over the years its meaning had evolved into a 'gathering' or 'coming together.' Of course, the expression powwow is now used by all Native American groups country wide and has been adopted by Americans for everyday use.

"All powwows are not the same. Some are very small (almost a family gathering) and others are huge affairs which attract hundreds of dancers and thousands of spectators. There are varied reasons for having a powwow. Many are held in honor or an event or to pay tribute to a member. Some raise money for scholarships. Groups may use proceeds to cover their operating expenses. Every attempt is made to keep admission cost down so that the powwow will continue to be a family program.

"Regardless of size or sponsorship, certain customs and traditions are observed. The music is the overriding theme. A group of men sit around a large drum. Their drum beat accompanies their singing. Frequently, the women stand behind the men and sing. In our area, women do not beat the drum. The beat of the drum is the heartbeat of the powwow. The singers are generally not called drummers but are referred to as singers. Occasionally, one singer will do a program with a drum and act as master of ceremonies.

"The formal powwow opens with a grand entry of participants in regalia. This is led by the chiefs and medicine people of the host group, followed by other chiefs, elders, medicine people, honored guests, traditional men dancers, feather dancers, women and children. Order of entry is determined by the host group and there are many variations of this sequence.

"Following the entry, flag songs and veteran's songs are sung. These are honoring songs and the spectators are asked to stand, remove their hats and remain quiet. Then a general program follows with dances of welcome, intertribal dances, sneak ups, and other favorites. There are other additional honoring songs, two step dances (done by couples)and round dances. The public is frequently invited to dance a round dance.

"It is important to remember that a powwow is not a show, nor is it a choreographed program. Most of the participants enjoy having spectators but the dance is still the central reason for being there, and the dancing frequently continues into the evening long after the public has left. To us a powwow is a gathering of family and friends, an opportunity to meet and exchange cultural ideas and plans, a method of teaching our children about this wonderful culture, and an opportunity to inform everyone that the Native American spirituality is alive and well and to thank the Creator for bringing us together.

"There are many traditions and rules of etiquette which are observed by spectators and participants. Space doesn't allow me to address these issues at this time - another article perhaps. However, if you will ask questions and listen to the master of ceremonies, you will enjoy the powwow and perhaps, we hope, experience the joy of reunion."

This article written by Whirling Thunder appeared in the Newsletter of the Robbins Museum of Anthropology – Middleborough, Massachusetts – February 1993

AMERICAN INDIAN FEDERATION

One of the original reasons for attempting to put all of these experiences on paper was to illustrate how Powwows have changed over the years and I think that the Lafayette Powwow is the perfect "before" Powwow. The Lafayette group maintained the old time flavor of Eastern Powwow activity. Most of the dancing was done as specialty-type dances. There was a Buffalo Dance, Partridge Dance, Warrior's Dance, Challenge Dance, Feather Dance, Spear Dance, Woman's Dance, and the Corn Dance. These specialty dances were interspersed with general dancing in which all would participate. The Master of Ceremonies conducted the program. He provided the music and his main responsibility was to make each and every dancer look good.

As Powwows evolved, you could see the use of singing groups with many singers rather than a sole Master of Ceremonies who also sang and provided the music. Additionally, there would be more general dancing and the Fancy Dance, Jingle Dance, and the Fancy Shawl Dance became the specialty dances of choice. These specialty dances frequently were performed by more than one person.

The American Indian Federation in the Lafayette section of North Kingstown, Rhode Island, was founded in 1931 and was fully chartered under the laws of Rhode Island. The Federation's first Powwow was held in 1931, and there have been Powwows held every year through at least 1990. As other intertribal groups came into being, Powwows became more frequent. With the increase of groups and the busy lifestyle in general, it became more difficult to attract and keep members.

Membership waned and events became an ever increasing burden for those who were trying to keep it all together.

Some of the early members of the American Indian Federation were Chief Leading Canoe (Charlie Wells), Princess Nashaweena (Sadie Barrie), John the Bear (Johnny Martin), Red Bird (Clarence Smith), Anna Clear Water (Anna Riccitelli) and John Riccitelli. During the 30's and 40's, when the organization was very active, the hall, located at 1 Indian Street, at the corner of King Street, was used all year round for monthly meetings. The wood stove kept the hall warm for these meetings, but eventually heating in this manner became impractical and when necessary, winter meetings were held in members' homes. As a means of fundraising, frequent socials were held which consisted mainly of ham and bean suppers, turkey suppers, and the strawberry festival. Members of the organization supported these functions and the public was also invited. These were very popular events.

In the early 1970's, the Federation's meetings were held monthly from late April through October. Winter meetings were not held every month but we held a Thanksgiving feast at a member's home. These were always most memorable. Indian organizations were, and still are family oriented. The Native culture holds the family in high esteem and emphasizes this basic structure. When I became a member of Lafayette, my entire family became members. Lafayette, like most other organizations in the late 1960's, consisted of tribal members and associate members. Associate members did not participate in voting but were welcome as full members in every other sense. Our children benefited tremendously from belonging to these intertribal organizations.

The Indian Hall was a former church - a small building

probably 40′ wide by 60′ deep. It consisted of a large hall, two restrooms and a small kitchen. The kitchen served us very well. A good sized table was always loaded with food for refreshments after the meetings. Coffee was made and hot tea was served and generally the conversation and the fellowship lasted longer than the meeting.

The interior of the hall was unfinished. It was not plastered and did not have a sheet rock covering. The studs were exposed. There was a single chimney and one very large wood stove. At the time we joined the organization this stove was no longer used. At the end of the hall there was a very small platform, probably only 6′ x 8′ and elevated about 10″ above the floor. A desk on the platform was flanked by two stanchions. One stanchion held the American Flag and the other held the state flag of Rhode Island. Two chairs at the desk were used by the Squaw Sachem and the Chief when meetings were being conducted.

When we joined the Federation, there was a big sign on the front of this desk, which faced the members when a meeting was being conducted. It was a white sign with 6″ high blue lettering that said "First Prize Most Approriate". Unfortunately, the word "Appropriate" was spelled incorrectly. The sign had graced a float, sponsored by the Federation, in a parade in the city of Attleboro, Massachusetts. An Indian motif was used for the float and many of the members rode on the float in the parade. They won a prize – obviously for being the most appropriate! The sign was brought back to the hall as a souvenir of the event, incorrect spelling and all. We knew that it was spelled incorrectly but for some reason the sign was never removed in all the years which I held membership in the American Indian Federation. Big

Thunder (Fred Reynolds) said, "It was Attleboro's fault that the spelling was incorrect."

Paul and Princess Nashaweena with the infamous sign at a Lafayette meeting

The walls of the hall were decorated with various artifacts, bows and arrows, a deer head trophy, painted hides, and a copy of each of the fliers for the Powwows starting from 1935. Unfortunately squirrels inhabited the hall from time to time and on one of their visits they completely destroyed all of the fliers, which had been so carefully preserved and displayed.

The hall itself had been given to Princess Nashaweena (Sadie Barrie), Squaw Sachem, in the late 30's or early 40's. A gentleman from the Fall River, Massachusetts area deeded it to Princess Nashaweena with the understanding that it would be used as an Indian Hall or as a church. The Federation continued to use the hall after Princess Nashaweena's passing.

In intertribal Native groups, the Squaw Sachem is a

respected female Elder who is looked to for guidance and honored for her wisdom. Once granted this position, the Squaw Sachem holds it for the balance of her life. She is revered and respected by the members of the group. There may be subtle differences in the role among groups, but the basics are the same. Princess Nashaweena certainly fulfilled this role with dignity and ease.

The grounds were very small and the entire area was shaded, mostly by oak trees and some maples. One side of the lot was bordered by an old, stone wall. Behind this wall was a beautifully wooded area, which was completely undeveloped. One of the other sides had a wire fence, not a cyclone fence, but a wire fence, which separated it from neighboring property. Although small, it was a very peaceful area and a very comfortable place to be.

Princess Winona had told me that during World War II Powwows were not held. Princess Nashaweena advised me that there was a Powwow or an observance every year without exception. Of course, during the war years many of those who would ordinarily be participating were in the Service and their families were otherwise engaged in the war effort. Many Powwows and other Indian activities were curtailed during World War II.

The necessary equipment for the annual Powwow was stored in the hall. Tipi poles and ladders were stored in the cellar while tipis and electronic equipment were stored in the main hall. A rope had been used for a number of years to delineate the dance circle during the Powwow. Many years ago large screw eyes had been put in certain trees and the rope was laced through these screw eyes. You started the rope at a certain tree and it was the exact length needed to go back to its starting point. The rope could be taken off a hook so that participants could enter the circle. Powwows at that time, and even now, for the most part are set up with some sort of rope or ribbon arrangement to mark off the circle. Sometimes bales of hay are used. In the case of Lafayette, the grounds were so small that it was necessary to rope off the circle to provide adequate dancing space.

A microphone was used and two large, old (certainly not antique) but certainly old, loud speakers were placed high in the trees and the sound of the music and voices could be heard throughout the entire neighborhood.

It was necessary for the vendors to drive their automobiles onto the grounds, unload their wares, set up their tables, and then the autos had to be taken off site. Parking was always a problem even into the 60's and 70's. Fortunately, we didn't see people with large campers and huge vending setups. Most of us had several card tables. These were covered with "Indian" blankets, which were cotton blankets sold by many department stores and 5 & 10 cent stores at that time. Generally speaking, none of the vendors had any money. When we purchased a used station wagon, we were one of the more fortunate ones, in that we were able to bring more of our goods to the Powwow. There was room for only 9 or 10 vendors to set up around the perimeter.

Princess Nashaweena did not drive. Often Mae Carr of Saunderstown, Rhode Island, who had held the post of secretary of the Federation for many years, drove Princess Nashaweena to various functions. When meetings were held in the winter months, I usually drove to North Kingstown to pick up Mae and Princess Nashaweena and then drove them to wherever the meeting was being held. Princess

Nashaweena's husband Jim was ill and was not able to leave the house. We would always go in and talk with Jim for a few minutes until Princess Nashaweena was ready to leave. Frequently one or two or more of our children went along for this ride and we always enjoyed having Princess Nashaweena and Mae with us. We frequently held meetings at our house but we also were welcomed at other members' homes.

Active membership when we joined was probably 30—35 people. However, there were at least 40 or more inactive members who were unable to attend meetings but did assist us and participate in the annual Powwow. When we first joined the organization, a man named Gray Fox was the Chief. His Christian name escapes me.

While many Native children are named at a very young age, not all are. I had always used my Christian name but Princess Nashaweena thought that I should be properly named. After a period of serious reflection she named me Whirling Thunder and this is the name I carried throughout the rest of my life. Princess Nashawena's reasoning was the high level of activity in my life. She thought that my many and varied activities kept me "whirling."

After Gray Fox, Silver Cloud (Harry Jacques) became Chief and held that post for quite some time. After Silver Cloud resigned, Princess Nashaweena asked me to run for chief to replace him. I was reluctant to do this for many reasons; raising six kids required a lot of time and effort. I was commuting from Attleboro to Boston at the time, as well as teaching two nights a week. Additionally, we made frequent trips to Bristol, Rhode Island to visit my Aunt Doris who was not well. Our children were involved with Boy Scouts and Girl Scouts, track, and school activities, and spare time was at a premium. I also felt that the post should go to a long time member. Princess Nashaweena invited me to come to her home one evening to talk and she had called Bright Canoe (John Diabo) who drove up from Brooklyn, NY to help her persuade me to take the post. Long story short - I was elected Chief and held the post for seven or eight years. It was a most rewarding experience and yet most frustrating.

Princess Nashaweena, who had been Squaw Sachem for many years, was very accustomed to doing things her way and was very reluctant to accept new members in the organization. She was also reluctant to accept new ideas and adapt to new ways of doing things. Her comment was, "Well, we tried that before and it didn't work." Or, "We tried that before and we didn't enjoy it." Although we had many difficult times during these years it was an enriching time.

The Lafayette Powwow had a strong reputation and we worked hard to maintain the Powwow as a quality historic event. Many assumed that the organization made a great deal of money at Powwows. On the contrary, as Princess Nashaweena aged, I learned that she had used her own money to pay Powwow expenses for many years.

The group's main activity was to conduct an annual Powwow to help maintain a strong fellowship. We now know from experience that it takes about a year to plan for a Powwow because there are many things that need to be done. One of the big expenses was the hiring of a local police officer to direct traffic. He would also keep in radio contact with the station in case we needed any emergency assistance.

Princess Nashaweena worked extremely hard contacting people and working with the press. She was very well known and was always able to have an invited dignitary attend her event. Many governors of the State of Rhode Island attended the Powwows and brought their greetings. Senators John O. Pastore and Claiborn Pell were frequently in attendance. The local elected officials usually came to mingle with the spectators. The town government was most solicitous of Princess Nashaweena. Since its inception, the Lafayette Powwow has been an area tourist attraction.

One year, our good friend Paul Sleeping Wolf (Paul Norback), who was Mohawk, was introduced by Princess Nashaweena to Rhode Island Governor Richard Garrahy. The Governor was dressed in a light weight suit with a shirt and tie and was accompanied by a driver who was casually dressed and did not fit the mold of a politician. As Princess Nashaweena introduced Sleeping Wolf to the Governor, Sleeping Wolf looked at the driver, put out his hand, shook the driver's hand and said, "It is a pleasure to meet you, Governor Garrahy." He then turned to the Governor and said, "It was nice of you to drive Governor Garrahy today." This was an indication of Sleeping Wolf's subtle distain for politicians and anyone in power. Paul Sleeping Wolf could pull these things off. He was very highly educated and taught school for many years. His way with words enabled him to say things in an acceptable way - had someone else used them they may have been offensive. Sleeping Wolf left people unsure whether they had been congratulated or offended.

For a Powwow participant, one of the most exciting parts of the event is what we now call Grand Entry. In the past, it was called a parade. At Lafayette it was called the "Grand Parade" and was a most effective way to attract many people to the Powwow. All of the participants in regalia would congregate

Ben Massey and Paul discussing the program, Lafayette Powwow

in front of Indian Hall. Entire families, in their most elaborate outfits, would be lined up in accordance with the Squaw Sachem's (Princess Nashaweena's) line of march.

Bright Canoe and Ben Massey would lead the line, singing all the way down to the corner, which was probably a quarter of a mile away, past all of the homes on the street. Frequently there would be a shut-in or ill person at one of the homes and everyone would stop there. The singing would continue and we would put on a short dance for the people looking out their windows. All the time this parade was going on, people were walking up the street in the opposite direction, of course, to attend the Powwow. The line of colorfully dressed dancers would proceed down to the end of the street to Route 102. This was a semi-major roadway and the parade, of course, would attract travelers on the way to the many beaches in South County, Rhode Island. Bright Canoe would walk in a large circle in the center of the roadway, blocking traffic. All of the dancers would file by, and we would return to Indian Hall, usually followed by many curious and interested people. It was a very festive event. As we returned to the Powwow grounds, we filed into the circle and Ben Massey sang a Navajo Flag Song. Two or three veterans would always be at the flagpole with the folded colors. The flag would be raised briskly to the strains of the music. Immediately following the Flag Song, the Powwow would commence.

Bright Canoe had a traditional pipe, which was quite long and well decorated. In the early days, a pipe ceremony was usually done at the beginning of the program by the Chief or Medicine Man, at the center of the circle. The simplicity, tradition, and narration of the ceremony always thrilled the audience and was a highlight of any program. After the Chief completed presenting the pipe to the four directions, he carried the pipe to the other dancers. Each man would place a hand on the stem to receive its blessing and the Chief or Medicine Man would place the bowl of the pipe upon the left shoulder of the women and children.

In more recent years, the pipe ceremony is seldom done in public. Many traditional people feel that it is a religious ceremony and should only be performed privately during our own ceremonies. Although I can certainly see the reason for this, I have participated in and narrated some Powwows at which the pipe is brought into the circle.

In the 1980's it became customary to bring many Chiefs and Medicine Men into the circle, where they would individually perform the pipe ceremony. As this procedure evolved, it became almost a common event or an opportunity to elevate the ego of the participants and the sanctity of the ceremony was diminished. The ceremony would last so long that the audience lost interest. The pipe ceremony now is generally done by a single person and seldom in Powwow circles.

Many of the individual dances were, what we called when I was young, an "I saw" dance. Frequently they were done in pantomime, and they would tell a story. For example a single

Chief Bright Canoe, Princess Nashaweena, Louie Deer,
Paul, and Ben Massey at Lafayette Powwow, 1980

dancer would perform a Hunting Dance in pantomime and the audience would use their imagination. This dance and several others are described more completely in subsequent chapters.

A few of the regular participants over the years were Mohawk people from the reservation. One such couple was Angus and Annie Marquis, who came from Caughnawaga. They had a souvenir booth. In our earlier days at Lafayette, Angus was the Veterans' Coordinator. It was his responsibility to make sure that the ropes had been replaced on the flag pole, that a flag was properly presented, and that two veterans were available to raise the flag at the beginning of the Powwow to the strains of the Flag Song. Although Angus was Canadian he probably had dual citizenship, as he had served in the United States Military. He was looked upon with great respect.

As years passed and Angus and his wife retired to the

Reserve, our friend Twin Skies (Louie Deer), took over the honor of being Veterans' Coordinator. Louie had served in the United States Navy. He was the guardian of the flag at all of the Powwows he attended. He would raise the flag at the beginning of each event and lower it at the close of the day. I was honored to be asked to assist him. For many years, Louie and I performed this service around New England and in New York.

Louie Deer and Paul tightening the rope
on the flag pole

During the last thirty-five to forty years, I have been intrigued by the Eastern dancers' practice of leaving the circle and how they do not remain in the circle when not dancing. I often wonder if perhaps the origin of this might have occurred at the Lafayette Powwow grounds. When we first came into the circle from the Grand Parade, a committee person would unhook the rope from the tree and we would file into the circle and space ourselves as evenly as we could around the perimeter of the dance circle. Of course, this made it difficult for the spectators to see clearly. Gradually we would move toward the entrance and stand closer together until finally we would leave the circle in order to permit the spectators to witness the dances taking place. It was always important to us to have those who were interested in the culture see what was going on – especially the children.

As Master of Ceremonies, I have encouraged dancers to remain in the dance circle but Eastern dancers invariably will leave between dances even when the spectators are able to see clearly what is going on.

Many years have passed and we frequently see Western style Powwows being put on in this area. Western style Powwows traditionally supply benches or chairs inside the circle. These benches are reserved for dancers and their families. It is customary for the dancer or family to place a blanket on that portion of the bench upon which they will be seated and it is a breach of etiquette to sit on anyone else's blanket. The result of this is of course, that the Western dancer is very comfortable sitting on the bench when he or she is not dancing and the Eastern dancer will leave the circle.

There are many differences in tradition between the Western and Eastern style programs. Unfortunately this creates some confusion at times and is probably resolved by the "when in Rome, do as the Romans do" concept. The host group will determine which tradition will be followed. I personally feel that chairs or benches within the circle are most acceptable and contribute to a much more intimate Powwow. However, after becoming accustomed to leaving the circle for so many years, I find it difficult to always sit down in the circle.

Even between dances, most Eastern people will leave the circle and come back in for the next dance. We see more and more people however, who do not hesitate to sit on the benches or stay in the circle from one dance to the next. At the conclusion of a song, I will generally stand off to the side within the circle until the Master of Ceremonies announces the next song. Depending upon the song, I will either dance or walk clockwise around the circle and leave by the east entrance.

The Lafayette Powwow was conducted by Bright Canoe, who was active in the New York area. He provided this event with a "built-in Powwow" group of probably 25 - 30 people. Before our affiliation with the organization, the group would come up from New York on Friday night and stay at Princess Nashaweena's house Friday and Saturday nights. At that time she owned a large home in Warwick, Rhode Island and the New York contingent would spend the nights and enjoy late evening meals with Princess Nashaweena. Later, after Princess Nashaweena had sold that large house and she and her husband had retired to a very small house on Frenchtown Road in North Kingstown, she did not have room to put all of these people up and they stayed in local motels.

The music was always provided by Bright Canoe and Ben Massey. They were ideal partners. They knew the same songs, which they sang very beautifully, and each had some of their own traditional songs, which they would sing solo. Ben Massey was a Navajo and brought music of the Southwest, which blended very well with the Northeastern songs. Most of the people who traveled with Bright Canoe were Mohawks from the Brooklyn, New York and Manhattan area. There were also some Shinnecocks from Long Island.

Other dancers from the New England area attended as well.

Because it was a two-day Powwow, and there were no camping facilities at Indian Hall, most area people commuted to their homes Saturday evening or went to one of the many campgrounds or motels in the area.

I was told once that the Mohawk people had many years ago been called "Circus Indians." This was not a derogatory term, but rather a way of describing them because they traveled extensively to put on dance programs at Powwows. They had been brought up doing this, learning this way of life from their parents. As we have found over the years, the Powwow experience becomes a part of the individual. I guess it is in our blood. We are most content and most happy when we are experiencing those things which happen at a Powwow.

One of the specialty dances at Lafayette was done by a man on the circuit who performed with the use of a bull whip. He would go out to the center of the circle and snap the whip a few times. This would alert the audience and attract their attention to his skill. At this point, Louie Deer would step out into the circle with a feather which was four to six inches long, hold the feather out in front of him, and our bull whip champion would snap the whip three or four times. With much fanfare he would pull the feather from Louie's hand. To attract more attention, a shorter feather would then be held out, sometimes by a somewhat reluctant volunteer. Then to heighten the interest, Louie would hold a feather, bend over, and display the feather between his legs. Again, with much fanfare, the bull whip would crack and the feather would be withdrawn from Louie's hand. The next part required much expertise on the part of the Master of Ceremonies, although he did not involve himself either with the whip or the feather. The Master of Ceremonies would announce dramatically that the next trick would be to have the bull whip snap the feather from Louie's mouth. Our friend Louie would usually play this up to the delight of the audience by taking a very small, short fluff and placing it in his mouth. The problem was that the feather was so small that it was obvious to the audience that Louie's nose protruded further out than the feather (a potential catastrophe). Again, with much fanfare and speculation, the audience would either agree that it could be done or were quick to indicate that it couldn't be done. The whip man would snap the bull whip underhanded so that the whip would snatch the fluff from below. The spectators would hold their breath, the whip would snap and Louie, timing it perfectly, would exhale very quickly and the feather flowed from his mouth and floated to the ground. The whole thing was so fast, you couldn't actually tell whether the whip had taken out the feather, or whether Louie had decided to save his nose. It was done so cleverly that the spectators were amazed and impressed. It was a great crowd pleaser.

In the years before political correctness (and liability) became a factor, there were some skilled tomahawk throwers who could, in a safe area of the Powwow grounds, set up a log target and offer the spectators an opportunity to try their hand at throwing the tomahawk. It wasn't unusual to have a straw target set up and be able to teach people the archery basics as well.

This group of Mohawks from the New York area continued to form the basis of this Powwow. Bright Canoe was the leader and he selected people based upon their interest in participating, of course, and on their ability to offer dancing, crafts, or demonstrations. Many of the people who traveled with him had been doing it for years. They were all either related or very friendly. The young people came with their parents and this groomed future participants. The children were brought up in this atmosphere. Most of them are still on the Powwow circuit today and although for various reasons they may not be as involved as they were as children, the spirit seems to remain in them. Some of the people who traveled with Bright Canoe on a regular basis do merit recognition in this document. I will try to introduce them to the reader.

Most charismatic, outgoing, and knowledgeable, Bright Canoe lived in the New York City area with his wife, Minnie. Minnie operated the trader's stand when Bright Canoe was in the circle. He was a great singer and had a very strong voice and knowledge of the old songs. The arrangements have been somewhat altered, but we still on occasion hear these songs and I have heard music from the West which contains variations of the old Eastern music. Minnie did have an Indian name and it was not translatable into English. I am not sure how that could happen but I have been assured that it did, indeed. Minnie was not only an excellent bead worker but she did a lot of the leatherwork and the beading on outfits of the dancers in the group.

Ben Massey was Navajo. He and Bright Canoe frequently traveled and did programs together. Where Bright Canoe's voice was very strong, Ben's voice tended to be a little more melodic. Their two styles complemented each other. Ben could carry some of the program and sing some of the songs, giving Bright Canoe an opportunity to rest. They were good dancers as well. When they were together, they could rotate the singing schedule to afford the audience an opportunity to see each of them in a solo dance. This was always thrilling and exciting. Ben's wife, Emma, traveled with him and at Lafayette, she and her sister ran the kitchen.

Louie's wife, Green Leaf (Louise Deer), participated in the Grand Entry and performed at least two specialty dances at each performance. In addition, Louise was in charge of their business. Louie and Louise traveled all over Canada and the United States to purchase quality beadwork, quillwork, jewelry and pottery to sell at Powwows. Many of their wares were made at Caughnawaga and consisted of the old "built up" beadwork styles, which at one point had almost been lost to us. They would also have hundreds of handmade necklaces to offer for sale. These were made from sterling silver, beads, leather, kernels of corn, or wood carvings. It was a pleasure to view their wares which were always first quality and very traditional.

The first thing an Indian trader had to do was to set up his or her stand. We all had various forms of tarpaulins, some of them quite flimsy and apt to blow over with the slightest breeze. Lou and Louise always carried a very large, substantial canopy arrangement. The overhead of the canopy was just as tight as a drum, with numerous poles to hold it up, guy lines with very fancy knots and strong, sturdy pegs to hold the lines in place. This ability to tie great knots may have been a product of Louie's service in the United States Navy. In windy or rainy weather their booth was always warm, dry, and protected. In those days, it was not uncommon for Powwows to run into the evening, so they always had three or four lanterns which they suspended from the ridge poles to provide light and some warmth.

One time, setting up at Lafayette, their tarpaulin was in place, their tables were in place, and Louise was trying to cover the tables with the traditional blankets. The wind just would not cooperate, so Louie went over to the broken-down stone wall that bordered the property and got four small rocks to anchor the blankets so that the wind would not blow them off. A young mother and her daughter came along, took one look at the rocks and the mother said, "Are those Indian rocks?" Louise, who could be very serious, looked her right in the eye and said, "Yes, they are." The woman asked the price to which Louise replied, "Two dollars each." The lady said she would take three of the rocks. At this point Louise started to laugh. We joked about that for the rest of the Powwow. It was Louie's

Princess Winona and the Blanket Dance at the Lafayette Powwow

suggestion that if we had a big crowd for the balance of the weekend, we could sell the whole stone wall.

In those days, the Hickman family came from New York and set up. Little Word (Evelyn Hickman), Louie Deer's sister, was a dancer. She and Louise frequently performed a Woman's Dance. All of the people who sold from their stands were also dancers. It was customary and required that all people wear their Indian outfits while working their stands and that they would participate in any dances which the Master of Ceremonies would request of them.

For many years, the Cloud family came from New York to the Powwow. Although the parents were dancing only on a limited basis at that time, their son, Owl Feather, was one of the best dancers in New England. His Eastern style dancing was a forerunner of what later became known as the Fancy Dance. He was very energetic, stood very straight in the circle and was a tremendous crowd pleaser. This family was related to Chief Strong Horse (Ken Smith) of the Narragansett Nation.

Princess Winona and her sister, Quequella (Winifred), would set up at a prime location at the entrance to the grounds. They had probably 10′ or more for their tables and in the fashion of the day, covered them with the light weight "Indian Blankets." A series of umbrellas tied to the tables provided a limited amount of shade. Princess Winona participated in every dance program. Her specialty was the Blanket Dance, which is not to be confused with the Blanket Dance you see today. Eastern Blanket Dance was an older version done with a blanket, or modified shawl, with very short fringe. It told the story of a young maiden seeking a husband. Princess Winona danced during the intertribal numbers and came to the microphone on occasion to give a demonstration of Indian sign language.

The grounds were small and we had to strictly reserve and limit the number of traders. Our selling duties fell upon Harriett and the children, who always attended, although Harriett was the mainstay at the booth because the kids danced as often as they were able. Dancing in the circle was their favorite thing to do. Our dancers were Gray Hawk (Andy), One Feather (Chris), Brown Bear (Dan), Eyes That Shine (Ed) and Popshela (Faith). Our eldest, Betsey, although not a dancer, assisted in many ways both at Powwows and at home with regalia construction. Tall Oak (John Neidijadlo) a Penacook and a Federation member, set up on occasion, as did Chief Strong Horse (Ken Smith), a Narragansett.

Tall Oak (John Neidijadlo), 1980, a kind and generous man

Rounding out the traders, but just as important I guess, was a gentleman who showed up very early on the first Powwow day every year, at the invitation of Princess Nashaweena. He came in with a popcorn truck and parked at the side of the hall. He did a land office business. It seems the only time we ever saw the popcorn man was at Lafayette Powwow. He had been doing it for a number of years and was always most generous with a donation for the group at the end of the festivities.

There were other dancers who participated in the Powwow. Coming from New York was Joe Joseph and his wife Pat, who put on a Partridge Dance. This was narrated by Bright Canoe and was a story about a male and female partridge and their efforts to attract attention to themselves.

Louie Deer was always a Powwow favorite. His solo dances were superb, his enthusiasm infectious. When he was dancing in a very serious fashion, the audience would start to clap in

Chief Strong Horse dancing with Ben Massey providing the music - Martin Star and Clear Sky sitting in the background

unison with the drum. By the time he finished his solo, the audience would be really excited.

Princess Anna Clearwater at an early Lafayette Powwow

Princess Anna Clearwater (Anna Riccitelli) lived in Rhode Island and was a member of the organization. She had a beautiful white leather dress with beadwork. Even in her later years, she did a very graceful Woman's Dance. When we could persuade her, she would come to the microphone and talk to the audience. Anna Clearwater and her brother had been taken to Carlisle Indian School in Pennsylvania when they were young. At the school, they found very quickly that looking Native and speaking only the Native language were not acceptable. They were punished and brutally treated because of their Indianess. Anna's brother ran away from the school, Anna remained at the school throughout most of her childhood.

Another member of the American Indian Federation was Princess Morning Star (Marion Fisher), who lived in Wrentham, Massachusetts. Occasionally, it was necessary that I go to her home to visit or do some business for the Federation. The boys were always eager to go with me on these trips since Marion had a big black crow which had the run of the house and would talk if it was in the right mood. It was fascinating to watch that bird in action. Marion later became a charter member of the Wollomonuppoag Indian Council.

One of the dancers who had traveled with Bright Canoe extensively was Ken House. Ken was in the Military at the time so was not always available for programs. He is Oneida and his Indian name is very difficult to pronounce. Bright Canoe was not at all adept at remembering names and if the name was complicated there was even less chance that he would remember it. He always introduced Ken as "My Oneida Friend." Ken would go out and do a stirring Fancy Dance. He was one of the first Fancy Dancers in the area. The Fancy Dance

Ken House, Andy, and Charlene Standing Bear discussing Ed's singing of Johnny Diabo's song, 2004

originated in other parts of the country and was not traditional to this area. However, Fancy Dances are now very much accepted.

We were reunited with Ken in 2004 and enjoyed his

company at Powwows in Massachusetts, Connecticut, Maine, New Hampshire and Vermont. One weekend, we put on a small program in Spencer, Massachusetts. Our son Eyes That Shine (Ed) had learned a lot of the songs that Johnny Diabo used to sing and we asked Eyes That Shine if he would do a Johnny Diabo song for the audience. Ken, who was standing next to our son Gray Hawk (Andy), leaned over and said, "Oh, that is great. I bet Johnny Diabo is turning over in his grave right now." Andy said, "No, he is probably out at the main gate collecting admissions." Johnny was a superb entertainer, a very kind and generous man, and a good businessman. The success of his many adventures in life and the opportunities he presented for all of us to participate in, all directly resulted from his good business sense. Regardless of how dedicated we may be as dancers and Powwow attendees, all of these things cost a lot of money. The people who have the ability to not only organize, but to handle the business aspects, are few and far between and Johnny Diabo made a lot of things possible.

An Elder, a Cherokee named Mohongtasse (phonetic spelling) was a very tall, thin man who wore a headdress with dark feathers in the Eastern style, a Seminole jacket, and leggings with geometric beadwork design on the sides. He was a regular at the Powwow, even though he was not doing a lot of dancing at the time because of his age. He shared his knowledge of the development of the Cherokee alphabet by Sequoya and the sadness of the Trail of Tears.

When Bright Canoe and Ben Massey were not able to get to Lafayette, we were fortunate to have Joe Star and Clear Sky and their very talented family who not only provided the music, but introduced the community to many Southwestern dances. They were accompanied by Orange Blossom (Esther

Mohongtasse in 1974. Note his Seminole jacket, Eastern style feather headdress and beaded apron and leggings

Sando who now is known as Esther Clear Sky) War Arrow (Steve Sando) and their children Karl, Tina, and Martin Little Star.

We had an old bass drum which had been given to our family. It had been repainted two or three times and prior to its final demise, had one head broken which we were unable to replace. The tone was not affected and our boys, who had done such a great job of learning the music over the years, were able to sing with the Elders and do an admirable and professional job.

In the 1980's, the use of a bass drum was traditional for singers of Northern music. I think that, without exception, all Northern drum groups in the area used a regular bass drum, such as those used in bands and orchestras. In fact, we were always checking the Want Ads in hopes of being able to purchase an inexpensive bass drum. Often we received donations of drums from bands which had discontinued using them or had purchased more updated drum equipment. The beaters, which had soft, furry heads, have now been replaced with harder, leather wrapped heads. The use of bass drums has disappeared from style and all of

Martin Star Sando dancing with Joe Star, Steve Sando and Wildcat at the drum. Note the old "band" type drum being used

the Northern and Southern singers now use a drum which has been made from a hollowed out log. Steer hides, elk, or buffalo hide is used on these drums.

There were so many wonderful people who attended Lafayette over the years that it is a joy to look through photo albums of pictures from the Powwows. There is always a face that appears or reappears and brings back happy memories of times when we danced together. Probably the most frequently photographed was Spotted Eagle (Ken Brown). He was a very dedicated dancer and loyal friend of Princess Nashaweena's, who showed up early each Powwow morning and frequently brought a friend with him. Over the years that I knew Spotted Eagle and during the many Powwows that we attended together, invariably the local newspapers would print Spotted

Eagle's picture in a prominent place in their coverage of the Powwow. Photographers could be at Powwows all day long and the picture that the editor would choose to publish would be of Spotted Eagle.

Four Moons (Don Brennan) attended for many years and danced his ever popular Flag Dance using the Indian Banner or Coup Stick. Don was always ready and willing to entertain and interview some of our visiting dignitaries. On one occasion he got into a lively discussion with Governor Richard Garrahy over the beach traffic that he encountered coming to the Powwow, suggesting that the Governor should build another highway to accommodate this traffic.

Chief Strong Horse (Ken Smith) was a very popular regular participant. He would occasionally sing a couple of songs. He was always ready with his Chief's Dance. Also, looking through some of the older pictures, I noticed that Chief Big Horn (Dennis Champagne) participated, although at that time I did not know him. Dennis was a past Chief of the Federation and later returned as Chief.

When I talk about the Lafayette Powwow, I am always reminded of our son, Ed's participation in one of them. He was a spectacular dancer and the crowd enjoyed watching him. When he was about six or seven, the Master of Ceremonies, Chief Bright Canoe, decided that there would be a young persons' dance contest, just for the kids and just for fun. Ed was very proud when he was selected as the winner and as he strutted across the dance circle acknowledging the applause, he backed into the open (unlit) fireplace. He was quite embarrassed and it was a humbling experience for him.

Whether a dancer attends one Powwow a season or many he is always welcome. These gatherings are a reunion of sorts, a time to catch up with old friends and make new ones. It is a wonderful place to be renewed and to find peace, a wonderful culture in which to raise children. One can find many positive role models who enjoy shared values amidst this rich culture.

NORTH AMERICAN INDIAN CLUB

As the Bullock family became more active in the American Indian Federation, we were invited by a number of its members to attend meetings of the North American Indian Club, which was chartered in Willimantic, Connecticut.

The Club had been organized for a number of years and was an active family organization. There was an excellent youth group and we encouraged our children to become involved. The Club met monthly in various locations in the Willimantic area. They were a well-respected Native organization in Connecticut and were known for sponsoring an annual Powwow which attracted dancers, vendors, and spectators from New England as well as New York and Pennsylvania. Iroquois people from New York and Canada were active in the group and many of them traveled a great distance just to attend meetings as well as the Powwow.

Our family's involvement in these Powwows was our introduction to the full scale Powwow. It was one of the first big Western style Powwows held in the New England area by a Native group. Frequently, prize money was awarded to participants who excelled in a particular style of dance. This was the first time we had come in contact with competition dancing. The children were able to take their fair share of prizes and prize money. We emphasized to the children that the love of dancing was more important than winning the competition. We did not want them to feel that the prime reason for attending dances was to win a prize. Today, we seldom enter competition dances and consider ourselves very fortunate to be able to dance our own style and not concern ourselves with the possible monetary rewards. I don't object to competition dancing and I feel that this is the best way to get a good assortment of great dancers assembled. Certainly many of our current Powwows would be much less interesting were it not for the competition.

On occasion, I am asked to act as a judge for competition dances and I will decline the offer if I know any of the dancers. Since we know many of them, the net result is I seldom act as a judge. I find it very difficult to judge a contest where there is a different style of dance, different tribal affiliations, or clothing representing different eras. The selection of a winner is very subjective. Once in a while we would have a contest for the youngsters or the tiny tots, and we invited the children come into the dance circle and practice their skills. In cases like this, every child won and the main purpose was to teach them the joy of the dance. We encouraged all children to get into the circle – it builds confidence and poise. This created a desire to have an outfit or to improve an existing outfit and to feel comfortable in front of an audience. The Master of Ceremonies would often comment that even though the performance or regalia may not have been perfect, it was a learning experience for the child.

When we joined the North American Indian Club most of the officers and members of the council were Eastern Indians and a majority of them were probably from Northern New England (Abenaki, Passamaquody, Penobscot, MicMac).

Intertribal organizations generally go through cycles when their slates of officers seem to come from a particular geographical area. Many of my friends had been active in the organization previously and Strong Horse and Ben Massey had contributed immensely to the success of the group.

I have always been fascinated by Indian names - fascinated with the originality and the beauty of the names. Naming itself is probably the subject of a book. Some names consist of two words i.e. Red Fox, or can be one word, Redfox. There are times a Native man may have a surname which is different from his brother's even though they have the same parents.

As the Powwow grew in popularity it was necessary to change locations to accommodate the increasing crowd. Indian food vendors were in regular attendance so that Native foods as well as American hamburgers and hot dogs were offered. Church leaders attended Sunday mornings for those people who wished to attend services. There was a very active Baha'i group affiliated with this club.

The singers were there because they loved the music and they loved to sing and any financial remuneration received at a Powwow was not enough to cover their out-of-pocket expenses. It is very demanding of the singers' time and to remain successful, they probably have a weekly practice as well as weekend Powwows. The reservation Indians are a bit more fortunate in that they are usually within a short driving distance of each other, making it easier to get together for practices. Usually singing groups in non-reservation areas travel many miles to get together.

There were a number of drums at the North American Indian Club events and unfortunately I have forgotten many of them. An outstanding group, however, was called the

Brooklyn Drum; obviously it was from Brooklyn, New York. They sang in the New England area frequently during the summer. The Star and Clear Sky family, which included Steve War Arrow, provided much of the music as well. The Painted Fan drum, led by Howard Hahn, was active in the mid 1970's. They hailed from Long Island, New York.

The Powwow programs were two day affairs (Saturday and Sunday) but the dancers and vendors usually left their home Friday after work and drove to the Powwow location. The most fun for many of us was to be on the grounds setting up our camp site on Friday evenings as our friends came in from various locations from late afternoon through early Saturday morning. All night long you could hear hammers driving in tent stakes - people setting up their tents and lodges, making campfires for warmth. And of course there was the constant socializing and greeting of people who had not seen each other since the previous year. We did not really plan to have a full night's sleep on those Fridays. It was just a wonderful experience to see all of our friends, set up our campsites and prepare for the Powwow. In the midst of all of this confusion and activity usually a singing group would arrive and set up their drum by the campfire and sing some songs to get themselves in voice and to foster a bit more enthusiasm and spirit for the Powwow.

Saturday morning usually found everybody sleeping late. It was always very difficult to get everyone moving, have breakfast, and prepare for the Powwow. All of the dancers in our family had to get their outfits ready, bustles assembled, roaches unwrapped, and be sure everything was ready for Grand Entry. Around 10 am the public started to come into the grounds. They paid a nominal fee at the gate and roamed around checking things out while listening to taped Native music.

Sometimes a drum would have a final practice while the vendors set up their tables. Grand Entry usually was held around noontime. At this Powwow, the term "Indian Time" was used or perhaps abused. "Indian Time" came to mean informal scheduling without reference to any particular clock. We have found over the years that while this term is used, we try not to abuse it. We try to adhere to the schedules as set up so that everyone will know what to expect. When a snafu occurs, we tend to use the term "Indian Time" to explain a change or delay in schedule.

The Powwow opened with the Master of Ceremonies announcing the Grand Entry. This would be followed by the Flag Song and the Veterans' Song. The colors, which were brought in during Grand Entry, would be posted and the dancing would begin.

This was a Western style Powwow and the program lasted all day and consisted primarily of intertribal dances. A Master of Ceremonies would keep the program going as smoothly as possible and the contest dances would be mixed in with the intertribal numbers so that those people who did not compete would get an ample amount of dance time.

A printed program was distributed to dancers and spectators alike. This included the times of contests in the various categories. Some of the categories included Tiny Tots, Young Girl, Young Boy, Fancy Dance, Warriors, and sometimes, a Seniors' or Elders' and perhaps a Women's Traditional. We did not see any Jingle dresses at this time as they had faded from popularity and did not come back for a number of years. There were very few specialty dances so many of the dances we did at Lafayette were not seen here. We did have the old Challenge Dance, which consisted of four men who placed themselves at the four directions and each in turn danced around the other three and attempted to make them lose their balance using all sorts of intricate dance steps. The object was to have the other dancer lose his balance without touching him. This was always a good crowd pleaser.

The Joe Star/Clear Sky family frequently did some of their Southwestern specialties, which presented a change in pace and style.

At suppertime, a break was called. The dancers would all return to their campsites and change into their street clothes. Most families brought food, which they cooked on their campfires. Of course some took advantage of the vendors' cook shacks, enjoying the Native and non-Native food offered there. Supper would be cleared away and the singers would go back to the circle first. The Calling Song was sung and all would go back to the circle – socializing on the outside or dancing on the inside. The singers would sing "49"songs which are a type of informal songs consisting of Round Dances, Stomp Dances, and general Powwow dancing. Very few participants remained in outfits, preferring the comfort and coolness of casual clothes.

Let me just say a few words about "49" songs. There are many different explanations of the origin of these songs and I will share one with you. It is said that 50 friends went off to war in the service of their country, promising to celebrate their safe return with song. Upon returning to their village a song was sung for each man in turn. Sadly, only 49 songs were sung. The 50th man did not survive the war.

Spectators were still very welcome on the grounds and

many of them sat around the circle socializing and were also welcome to come into the circle to participate in any of the "49" music. The drums would alternate so that all of the singers had an opportunity to sing. This would go on until 10 pm or later. Sometimes there was a strict curfew imposed by the neighborhood, so that the music would cease at 10 or 11 pm. The music of the drum carries for miles and miles, so was very disturbing to neighbors if the dance went on too late.

There was no formal program in the evening. It was strictly "49" music - Two Step, Round Dance, Stomp Dance and similar dances. If a group of singers was ready, they could do a song of their choice. When that song was over, there might be a few minutes before another drum began. As the evening wore on, the campfire was reduced almost to embers and the session would end. Families went back to their camp sites. The children were put to bed and the adults divided into small social groups, visiting, drinking coffee until the wee hours. After being so busy with the set up and confusion of Friday night and after dancing all day, sometimes in the hot sun, people were ready for a good night's sleep on Saturday evening. There were, however, some groups which elected to party noisily. Security people were called and generally they were able to quiet the noisemakers so that others could sleep. One night, a particular group was especially noisy and Star and Clear Sky were sleeping in that area in their camper. Joe Star was very active early in the morning, so he liked to go to bed early in the evening. Joe listened to the noise going on outside his camper and asked for quiet. The group quieted down for a brief time but as the conversation picked up in volume again and again, Joe went out asking for quiet so he could sleep. The third time he came out he made no effort to disguise his anger and left them with the threat that he would not tolerate it any longer. Regardless, the noise continued until very early the following morning.

Joe Star, never one to be outdone, was up as usual at 5:30 am and stood in front of the tent where the offending party goers were sound asleep. He pounded on a fry pan to wake them up saying that it was time to get up - it was Powwow time and they should know better than to keep people awake all night. Needless to say, they found out that Joe Star was a man of his word.

I mentioned briefly the calling of the security people. Most Powwows select a number of volunteers who serve as security for the event. It is their responsibility to see that problems do not arise, and also, to handle diplomatically whatever situation was brought to their attention. Some of the larger Powwows may have eight or ten security people who wear identifying tee shirts so that they will be identified. Sometimes they are EMTs who serve in a dual capacity and run the first aid station. Security and safety are prime considerations and they take their jobs very seriously.

Some of the Western Powwows utilize security personnel for the same purpose but also add an additional responsibility to assure that non-Indian visitors do not go into areas that are forbidden to them. They will also enforce the "no camera" regulation. A tip for people who may travel to reservations - always check very carefully and get permission to use a camera. When in doubt or lacking the proper authority, it is best to keep the camera secured in the trunk of your automobile.

The Sunday program usually attracted more spectators than on Saturday. The final dance contests were held, the finalists were selected by the judges (in private, of course), and the most popular contests were held. The Ladies' Traditional, the Men's Traditional and the Fancy Dance contests attracted the most people and enthusiasm. Runoffs were held in all categories and prizes and recognition were announced in the late afternoon. Sometimes monetary prizes were awarded; frequently a gift would be presented. Blankets were and continue to be the most popular prize given. Most contest dancers were awarded ribbons, which were personalized and would be worn with pride on the man's outfit or the women's shawl. When contestants signed up for the dance competition in their particular categories, a number would be assigned to them. This was in the form of heavy cardboard about 6″ x 6″ which would be attached to the dancer's regalia for the entire weekend. It would not be unusual to see many dancers in the circle with a number pinned to their clothing. This number was used by the judges as a means of identification.

Sometimes contest rules stipulated that the contestant must dance in each of the general dance sessions. Some Powwows required that a contestant be part of the Grand Entry for each and every program at the dance. This way, the judges could check each person's participation in the general events. The numbers identified each contestant.

Drum groups would also compete for prize money.

The formal program usually came to an end at 4:30 or 5 pm and Veterans were called upon to retire the colors. Final announcements were made and any further recognition of the winning dancers took place at this time.

Most families had a long ride home and had to be ready for work and school early on Monday morning, so the Sunday session did not go beyond 5 pm. Of course, campsites had to be taken down and campfires extinguished. Clothes and outfits were packed up, and goodbyes said. At this point everyone was tired. We would load our automobile with camping gear, outfits, vending tents, and trade goods and head for home.

The children were tired and hungry and the adults were exhausted and hungry. It was a ritual to stop for an evening bite on the way home. Of course, the conversation was always very lively. The enthusiasm that the kids had built up in the previous couple of days spilled over and they talked about the various events, contests, and various outfits they had seen, the people they had met, their favorite dancers and their favorite singers.

A great deal of talk would center around what one of the children was going to make, buy, or have made, in the line of regalia. We learned at this point and still know that we never finish working on regalia. It seems that the clothing would be worn-out or something we had seen needed to be copied. The term "regaliaitis" became a part of the Bullock vocabulary and the noise and the confusion of all the things they wanted to add to their regalia, on top of a very tiring weekend would make it necessary to say that they had a serious case of "regaliaitis." Finally, we would reach the point when we were "Powwowed out" and needed to come back to the "real world" of work and school.

Our day didn't end when we drove into our driveway since it was a must that we unload our car or van before going to bed. We had only one vehicle at this time and I needed an empty car on Monday morning. At times we would wake some or all of the children and although it was not their favorite part of the weekend, they cooperated with us by helping bring things into the house. It would be shower time and bedtime for all.

This became our life and we still remember with fondness those members and friends we met and the family weekends we enjoyed for a number of years. Most Powwows in the summertime are weekend Powwows; occasionally, a long holiday weekend afforded us the opportunity to spend three days.

In the colder weather of late fall, winter, and early spring our Powwows are held indoors and might only be one day events. A two day Powwow in the wintertime is frequently too expensive and the one day events continue to be good times for us.

Not only did we attend North American Indian Club Powwows, but we became very involved in the fabric of the organization. There were many social events, parades, and other get together opportunities, as well as monthly meetings. We became active on various committees and found that we were driving from Attleboro to Willimantic on almost a weekly basis. Additionally, I was elected a member of the Council, which required regular meetings and subcommittee meetings.

In 1976, one of the officers of the North American Indian Club was getting married and invited a large number of people from the Club to attend the wedding, requesting that we wear our Indian outfits. It was a beautiful wedding. The bride wore a traditional white gown and the groom wore a tuxedo, but the first two or three pews of attendees were dressed in their Indian finery. The minister was very enthusiastic about this wedding and had references within the ceremony about Native American traditions. He was so enthusiastic that he managed somehow to go out the side door of the church and run around to the front steps so that he could take pictures of the bride and groom leaving the church followed by a large contingent of Native Americans.

Directly across the street was a small village green where the spring flowers were at their prettiest. This was a favorite location for wedding photographs to be taken. Many photos still survive showing us in our finery – these photos reside in our album of happy memories.

We found that many of our Powwow friends participated in Thanksgiving feasts and periods of giving thanks. It was not unusual at all to receive a number of Thanksgiving cards at holiday time. It was not necessarily a traditional Thanksgiving (i.e. Pilgrims with buckle shoes, Natives in loin cloths) but an opportunity to celebrate the harvest. Traditional meals were held by most of the Native organizations. Although we were very accustomed to attending meetings where refreshments

Native guests at Little Giant's wedding in July of 1976

were served, it became a delightful custom to participate in these Thanksgiving festivities. The North American Indian Club was no exception to this and each year sponsored a "day of thanks" where family and friends participated in the celebration of the harvest. A traditional Thanksgiving dinner was always prepared and served. It became the social highlight of the season for many organizations of this kind.

Every traditional food was involved and either prepared on site or brought to the feast by attendees. Of course, it was a family affair as most Indian festivities are. It was always more interesting and more fun because so many family members and friends would attend, many of whom we had not seen for some time.

The North American Indian Club held a Thanksgiving meal at their November meeting. The American Indian Federation also had a Thanksgiving dinner (sometimes in later years, we hosted it at our home in Attleboro). The Bullock family was fortunate because we also had our family on Thanksgiving Day at our home. For a number of years, we enjoyed having three full Thanksgiving feasts each year. We think of these days as contributing so much to our family traditions and we value the spirit and friendship they encouraged.

The membership of the North American Indian Club decreased over the years for various reasons; Native activities became more common and people could find clubs and organizations and tribal groups closer to their home. At this particular time in our national history, there was much political unrest which threatened to spread into the Powwow arena in Connecticut. We shifted our Powwow focus to activities in the Massachusetts area.

We met many people through this group – our friends to

this day are some Mohawk people who were living in Brooklyn, New York and many Schaghicoke people from Long Island who found their way to the Powwow. Our friends Lou and Louise Deer attended at our invitation originally and continued their association for a number of years. It was around this time that we would see many Oneida families who attended the Powwows, but only on Sunday. The missionaries from the Seventh Day Adventist Church had spent a considerable amount of time with the Oneida people and as converts, the Oneidas would not participate in Powwows on Saturday. They confined their dancing and selling activities to Sunday only. An effort was made to accommodate these people so there would always be room for them if they were selling and exceptions were made for them in dance contests.

As we look back on our involvement in the North American Indian Club, we realize what a positive influence it had not only on our children, but on the entire family.

A very serious Paul with Princess Winona at the North American Indian Club

INDIAN LEAGUE OF THE AMERICAS

In the summer of 1970 the Bullock family decided to spend a week camping in the Bear Mountain, New York area. We had a very restful few days and visited the Plume Indian Museum and Craft Store in Monroe, New York. This trip to Plume brought back many memories of visits to Plume when it was located in New York City. I remembered the many times I journeyed to the 155 Lexington Avenue, New York City address to purchase Indian supplies, to visit with customers and to pester Mr. Luongo (as only an eager young boy could). I met, or met again, Mr. Lou Luongo at this time - unfortunately I don't think he remembered who I was from so many years earlier.

In 1986, the Wandering Bull, Inc would purchase the Plume Trading & Sales Co. and move the entire inventory to Attleboro, Massachusetts. Of course, in 1970 we had no idea that this venture would be in our future.

The next day we journeyed to the Indian League Powwow in Barryville, New York. What a trip that was! Breathtaking scenery awaited us as we drove along the Delaware River. We reached the town and turned off the highway, following Powwow signs which led us to a dirt driveway. We started up the driveway in our Volkswagen bus loaded with kids, camping gear, and enthusiasm. This driveway went up and up (we weren't sure the old bus would make it). We finally arrived at a grassy area where automobiles were being parked. There were huge busses, automobiles, campers, bicycles and people on foot all headed to the same location (up to the clouds it seemed). At the top of the hill we found that our friend Hungry

Horse was directing the vehicles to various parking areas. We had no sooner parked when the doors of our vehicle opened and our children went in six different directions to meet their friends.

Our 1970 VW Bus

The whole mountain seemed to be a series of terraces. There was one terrace reserved for parking. Up above that was another for dancing and a third terrace housed a building where souvenirs and refreshments could be purchased. All of the improvements and work on this site had been completed by League members (and what a lot of work that must have been!). Our main interest was the dance terrace which was not constructed in the form of a circle but was rather a large rectangular area. At one end was a singers' shade, which provided a space for the Master of Ceremonies and the drums. The Powwow featured afternoon and evening dancing. The Mohawk people were night dancers, so they would have two programs during the day and one later in the evening. The evening programs might last until 10:00 or 10:30 pm. In order to accommodate the nighttime programs, there were poles along the perimeter of the dance area. Wires strung between the poles carried electric lights for illumination.

The entire area was surrounded by traders' booths, which featured an unusual array of souvenirs and crafts. There were many unique Canadian crafts offered. The audience stayed well into the evening, enjoyed the dancing and spent time at the booths.

The Indian League Powwows were exciting. They were a thrill in every sense of the word. I guess the first thing that always struck us as being important was meeting all of the participants who had found their way to Barryville. We not only saw and met people from the Six Nations, (Mohawk, Oneida, Seneca, Onondaga, Cayuga, and Tuscarora), we met Navajo, Rappahonack, Shinnecock, Schaghticoke, Wampanoag, Seminole, Sioux, Delaware and many other tribes. It was thrilling to have so many people representing diverse cultures and tribes together in one place.

There was a Seminole named Ernie, who participated in many of the Indian League events. Often he appeared in full Seminole outfit complete with the basket type hat, long shirt and high leather boots. Ernie was a singer and a dancer and we understand that he was also a good cook.

Although we camped at a number of Powwows with our family, we chose to "motel it" at the Barryville Powwow. This was not as easy as it may sound. The area abounded in natural beauty but the commercial aspect trailed behind. There were several summer hotels in the area which had passed their glory days and one motel which we favored. Generally, our group consisted of Lou and Louise Deer, Louie's sisters Little Word (Evelyn Hickman) and Margie Larson, Johnny Diabo and his wife Minnie and our family of eight - enough to almost fill the one near-by motel. This motel consisted of two low buildings - one building featured air conditioning and the second offered television, so upon making a reservation one had to specify which amenity was desired. This motel also featured a restaurant, which made late evening meals easy. There were a few other restaurants in the area but none so handy for us.

The Powwow featured a series of specialty dances as well as general intertribal dancing. The first time I saw a Mosquito Dance was at the Barryville Powwow. Many years later (2010 or 2011) I was privileged to see 50 or 60 couples doing this dance in a gymnasium at Bridgewater State University in Massachusetts. This was choreographed by Annawon Weeden.

One of the outstanding features of the Barryville Powwow was the number of unique solo dances in their programs. Many of these specialty dances are no longer seen on the circuit.

HUNTER'S DANCE

One of the most popular dances was when a single male dancer would perform the Hunter's Dance, in pantomime. The Hunter's Dance told the story of a man going on the hunt. He first made sure his bow and arrows were ready. As he removed an arrow from his quiver, again in pantomime, he would notch it making sure the bow string was tight and that he was ready for the hunt. The next part of the dance showed him going through the woods, moving the brush aside, and coming to a stream, kneeling down, dipping his hands into the water, bringing them up to his mouth and drinking. It is necessary that he keep a wary eye and watch for the enemy. He goes further into the brush when he sees animal tracks in the soft earth – perhaps a deer, perhaps a moose. He has to very carefully check the tracks. Are they a new indentation in the ground or are they footprints from many days ago? All of a sudden through the brush, he spots a deer. He gets his bow ready, pulls an arrow from his quiver, sets it up and shoots the arrow into the heart of the deer. At this point it is important that he apologize to the spirit of the deer and perhaps do a short dance of victory. He would go up to the deer, remove the entrails, bury the entrails in the soft earth, again all in pantomime. Then he struggles to get the deer up on his shoulder and bring it home in jubilation – to celebrate his good luck with the Elders and share the animal with them. Again, all of this is done in pantomime, there are no weapons, nothing is done that would indicate that this is anything but a celebration and the possibility of being able to help the people in the village. All would share the food. The Master of Ceremonies would narrate this dance so that the public would understand what was happening, adding to the suspense and excitement.

Chief Broken Arrow (George Hopkins) was well known for the Hunter's Dance in the New England area. I don't believe that he ever danced at Barryville but I think his name belongs in this narrative.

Sometimes an elderly male would get out into the circle and do all of the moves of the Hunter's Dance, but maybe he danced a little bit slower and a little bit more deliberately – whatever the style, whatever the music, there is a place in every dance for someone who has a unique idea and style.

Over the years this Hunter's Dance has evolved into some of the popular dances of today like the Sneak-Up Dance. But this dance was originally part of the old pantomime dances. We may not see the old dances, but we see the outgrowth at every Powwow we attend.

BUFFALO DANCE

Four Moons (Don Brennan) and I participated frequently in the Buffalo Dance; again this was done in pantomime. A number of men were invited to come into the dance arena and dance in the style of the buffalo. They were dancing in a herd, bumping into each other occasionally and their hands swung before them toward the ground. Suddenly, on the opposite side of the arena, a brave with a spear (or coup stick) was dancing in his own style, enjoying the freedom of the dance, when he spots a herd of buffalo. He creeps up very cautiously and dances across the circle. It becomes apparent that the buffalo have spotted him as well. He brings the spear up and charges the herd stabbing one of the buffalo which falls to the ground. He approaches the buffalo and turns his spear so that the blunt end is placed against the heart of the animal - this is to ask forgiveness of the animal, to thank the Creator for allowing the hunt to be successful and to allow the animal to go peacefully into the Spirit-world. It is only then that the hunter dances a very rapid dance of victory, his knees in the air. He does all of these things which indicate that he is a successful hunter. Again, the excitement is heightened by the narration of the Master of Ceremonies.

MEN'S FANCY DANCE

One of the most popular dances was the Men's Fancy Dance. This involved some very fast dancing and intricate footwork. The Fancy Dancers created an entirely new style outfit. The long fur, which is attached just below the knees of the dancers, was originally goat fur but now they use Icelandic sheep. It is very long and sparkling white. These are still referred to as "goats," which may be a throwback to the original fur used. A pair of beaded moccasins, fancy aprons or breech clout, a fancy shirt (the more colorful the better), matching beaded harness, headband, and beaded belt, along

Chris doing the Fancy Dance

with two colorful back bustles make this a very distinctive regalia. Upon the head of the dancer is a hairpiece of deer tail and porcupine hair (a roach). A pair of gym shorts completes this outfit. The dancing is very fast and lively and much is made of the contest aspect of this dance.

LADIES' FANCY SHAWL DANCE

The young ladies were watching the young men dance. They were of the mind that they could dance just as fast and as intricately. We had the Men's Fancy Dance and then all of a sudden we had Ladies' Fancy Shawl Dance which incorporated some of the same moves, same steps, with the same music. It provided a lively opportunity for the girls and women to display their dance skills. This dance is now called the Ladies' Fancy Shawl Dance. The shawl is very colorful and the clothing beautiful.

LADIES' BLANKET DANCE

Some of the women danced the Traditional Blanket Dance–not to be confused with today's Blanket Dance which solicits donations from the audience to help reimburse the singers' expenses. The Traditional Blanket Dance is a courting dance and invites the women to show how they would dance to impress a would-be suitor. This dance utilizes a blanket rather than a shawl, and is now often seen as a competition dance.

Whippoorwill doing the Ladies' Blanket Dance

Wildcat at Lafayette Powwow

STOMP DANCE

Of particular interest was the Stomp Dance, in which a lead singer was followed by a single file of dancers. The singer's lead was followed by the dancers' response. This dance utilized bells and rattles, sometimes deer toes and dew claws. These Stomp Dances could go on for hours in this ideal mountain location- disturbing the neighbors was not a problem or concern in Barryville. I have commented elsewhere in this book that the Mohawk Indians were frequently called "Circus Indians." There was a good reason for this - for many years the Mohawk people participated in performances in circuses and carnivals - delighting audiences throughout the country. Many of our friends told us about these performances as well as performances at Sportsmen's Shows. These were family activities. In line with that, the Barryville Powwow certainly added "Circus Indians" to its repertoire since we were always trying to come up with a new idea or a new dance, or a variation of one of the older dances.

WARRIOR'S DANCE

We worked up a solo dance and it was my privilege and honor to be the "soloist." At that time, I had a long double trailer headdress and a five foot long coup stick (a coup stick is a long stick to which a number of long feathers are attached. It is usually decorated with red wool and is used sometimes in place of a spear. However, it is strictly a decorative piece.) We decided that I would do a solo dance with the double trailer headdress which reached almost to the ground and would imitate a Warrior's Dance. One time, when Louie Mofsie and

Paul charging the singers with a flurry of feathers,
Barryville, NY, 1984

the Thunderbird Dancers were providing the music, we decided to do a Warrior's Dance. I went out into the center of the circle with my double trailer headdress and my long coup stick. I danced very energetically - using the coup stick to its full advantage and did a lively imitation of a warrior in battle. But the singers decided that the Brave needed a little more exercise. The music and the singing went on and on and would not stop. I was getting tired - it was warm and I was waiting for the song to end. The singers went on and on and I became quite fatigued.

I danced down to the far end of the dance area and decided that the best way to end this dance would be to take the coup stick, bring it over my head and charge the singers. I planned to turn left or right just before I reached the singers' arbor and that would end the dance. I brought the coup stick up, held it as a spear, and charged the singers. This was at one of the August Powwows and the grass, which had been quite long at the beginning of the Powwow, had been bent over and flattened to the ground. As I charged the singers, the grass was very slippery, the temperature was very warm and my moccasins were slipping out behind me. I got within 10 or 12 feet of the singers. My body went faster than my moccasined feet and I sprawled onto the grass with the double trailer headdress trailing behind, the coup stick in my hand. I ended in a flurry, which is what I had planned to do, except not quite as dramatically! All you could see from the audience was 100 or more long feathers and the red fluffs. I was buried beneath the feathers, my arms outstretched, and the audience did not know quite what to make of the whole situation. Bright Canoe, who was not acting as Master of Ceremonies that day, rushed out, determined that I was okay and then went out into the middle of the area and announced in a loud voice, "He's okay folks. This is just part of the program." They picked me up and went on to the next dance number. This was probably a little too dramatic, but it did illustrate how we developed the dances and sometimes ended up with a surprise ending.

THE OLD MAN'S DANCE

Another dance that we would do was called an Old Man's Dance. The Master of Ceremonies, usually Bright Canoe, would spend a considerable amount of time at the microphone explaining how dancers, no matter how old, could still follow the music and perform. It was designed so that his introduction would go on and on and finally, to conclude the introduction, he would introduce an "old man" who had been selected to do the next dance. At this time he would call out for Whirling Thunder but Whirling Thunder, who was sitting in a chair, had gone to sleep. Other braves and women folk would come over to wake Whirling Thunder and get him to his feet and Bright Canoe would announce in glowing terms that this was the Old Man's Dance.

As you know we did a lot of pantomime dancing and when Bright Canoe looked at me, I indicated that my arm was really hurting, my back was almost broken and I would limp to show Bright Canoe and the audience how badly I felt and indicated that I should not do this particular dance. They persuaded me – the audience would clap their hands and Bright Canoe would go into his introduction with his tom-tom and start singing. I would start off very slowly, limp, hobble around the dance area and again show how unable I was to complete the proper steps. I would indicate that the music was much too fast and he would slow it down. Even though it was slower I would tell him it needed to be even slower and he then would say, "Oh, you want something like Guy Lombardo?" and I would make a motion as if I had a guitar or a violin in my hand and was strumming it. This good natured banter went on for a while

Paul dancing the Old Man's Dance

and then suddenly Bright Canoe would speed up his music and I would all of a sudden be following the drum and dancing very, very fast. The audience always enjoyed this and it always evoked enthusiastic applause from them.

TOMAHAWK DANCE

One of the people who traveled with us frequently was an Apache fellow named Red Deer (Billy Muniz). Prior to the performance, we asked a gentleman in the audience if he would cooperate with us by wearing a black wig for a short time. We told him, of course, what would happen during the dance. Red Deer was introduced and he would do a lively rendition of the Tomahawk Dance. He would dance about with his tomahawk. All of a sudden he would rush into the audience and reach down to pull the wig off the gentleman's head. Red Deer danced around with the wig as a type of victory dance. This was always a crowd pleaser and we would do it whenever Red Deer was with our group.

COURTING DANCE

One of the favorite dances at both Barryville Powwow and the American Indian Federation Powwow was the Courting Dance. This is an out-growth of the Partridge Dance. In the mid 1970's Clear Sky adapted the Partridge Dance to what we now call the Courting Dance. This is done by a young couple: the man is attempting to woo the young lady by impressing her with his skill as a dancer as well as with many wondrous gifts. The male dancer, using props such as a long beaded necklace, a silk scarf, and a mirror board, courts the female. The male dances and prances around the maiden who is ignoring him.

He shows off his best dance steps as the tempo of the music increases, while she continues to ignore him. He twirls the necklace as an enticement to her, tries to coax her with the silk scarf and still she pays no attention. Even his skill as a dancer does not impress her; she turns away and continues to plant her corn. Waving his fan does not attract her interest. He is totally confused since he has offered her so many wonderful items and shown her his best dance steps. She shows only a little bit of interest in him and he is mystified as to how to proceed. Then he thinks of his mirror board. He looks at himself in the mirror board and then shows it to her. She is amazed with what she sees; she smiles shyly and hands the board back to him. She takes her blanket from her arm and carefully folds it over both of them. They dance off together in jubilation. Joe and Pat Joseph frequently performed this dance at Barryville and often Wild Cat (Paul Cloud-Caruolo) and his wife Whippoorwill (Margaret Cloud-Caruolo) did it at the Federation Powwow in Lafayette, Rhode Island and at Topsfield Fair in Massachusetts.

TWO STEP

As the campfire burned itself out and the dancers were tired and the public realized that they had to get back to their own campsites or cottages, it was then that the Master of Ceremonies would call for a Two Step. A Two Step is a partner's dance. Some people describe it as a "follow the leader" dance. It is really much more than a"follow the leader" dance because there are many more considerations. First of all, there has to be enough space between each couple so that if the leader abruptly turns or reverses direction it will eliminate the possibility of having a pile up. The couple does not follow the leader but follows the couple immediately in front of them. There are many variations of this dance. It is really up to the lead couple who can be very creative.

The origin, we think, is in the Oklahoma area, when the natives watched the soldiers and their ladies dancing a type of grand march. This looked like a lot of fun and eventually the Natives adopted the dance, changed the music, changed the songs to their own language - sometimes with a little bit of English, and enjoyed the dance.

A sample of the Two Step

The Indian League of the Americas was formed in 1956 as far as I remember. The organization was headquartered in the Brooklyn, New York area and met regularly and at least once per year sponsored a huge dance which was well attended. It seemed as if every Mohawk in Brooklyn found their way to the Indian League dance. There was a large concentration of Mohawks in Brooklyn at that time. A large hall was rented and entire families would reserve a "table" thus insuring that the family would sit together. They would bring complete meals to eat as a family. Everyone was encouraged to attend and youngsters were also most welcome. An orchestra was hired and it supplied music for ballroom dancing for those who were so inclined. At intermission an Indian program was conducted by Bright Canoe. Our family was very fortunate to attend a number of these dances and participate in the programs. It was basically a dance program similar to that which would be put on at the Lafayette, Rhode Island Powwow. Louie Deer was always an audience favorite and when he did his solo dance, the audience would be standing on the chairs clapping and cheering, encouraging him to go on and on. These parties were very interesting and most fun and we (the family) were able to attend for four or five years. It was always a pleasure to drive to Brooklyn on a Friday evening and stay with Louie and Louise and help with the arrangements for Saturday evening. Our children all loved Louie and Louise and it was fun to spend time with them.

PRINCESS WINONA
04/15/1911 - 01/28/2003

Our Native American story would not be complete without devoting a considerable amount of time and space to this woman, who was a longtime friend. She attended our graduations, our weddings, funerals, holidays, and was a part of our social circle as well as being most influential in all of those wonderful Indian things. We considered her a member of our family.

This biographical information was obtained from Winona in 1995 when she was 84 years old and we were very impressed with her memory.

Princess Winona was born Winona Pearl Harmon on April 15, 1911 in Lisbon Falls, Maine. She was Androscoggin, Wyandot, Passamaquoddy, and Scottish/English. She was one of four children: a sister, QueQuella (Winifred Harmon) was a year and half older, and an older brother Vernon and younger brother Vance rounded out the family.

When she was about 8 years old the family relocated from Maine to Massachusetts, where they lived in the Millbury, Sutton, and Rockville areas. Her father was a textile worker and moved frequently from the Worcester area back to textile mills in Maine depending upon the available work.

At one point, the family was fortunate to be able to move to one of the company owned mill houses. They had to rely primarily upon public transportation and for the most part were able to walk from home to school to work.

Her mother died of scarlet fever and quinsy sore throat when Winona was about eleven years old. Her mother was in her early thirties.

Winona's father remarried and she and her stepmother had a good relationship. The family continued to shuffle between Maine and Massachusetts, depending upon the work. As soon as she was old enough, Winona went to work in one of the mills in Bramanville, Massachusetts. She had to walk back and forth from Sutton to Bramanville. She worked six days, 48- 50 hours a week, making $13.00 a week. She also did other chores to make money such as cooking, cleaning, ironing and working for some neighborhood people. She later got another job at the West End Thread Mill. She started work at 7 am, again walking back and forth from home. In those days the weekly pay was turned over to the parents. The money was used for the support of the family.

Her interest in her Native American background was fostered by her uncle, Teddy, who lived in Maine. He would take Winona into the woods and teach her about the trees and the animals. Winona spent a considerable amount of time with her uncle and he impressed upon her the importance of being Indian. That was his way and he hoped that Winona would follow the Native trail.

Winona married Gilbert Hendrickson when she was about 20 years old. Her son, Whirling Star (Gilbert) was born in 1935 and Little Winona (June) was born in 1938. Winona was divorced from Gibby in 1945. She later married Charles Baroni.

Winona had a friend named Hank who introduced her to a group in Rhode Island, which happened to be the American Indian Federation. He also brought her to attend some events, held on the Mohawk Trail. She called him Crazy Hank and apparently he was instrumental in getting her to some of these events. When she joined Lafayette, she had not done much craftwork. But she was very interested in craftwork and started doing beadwork, making moccasins and making, dressing and decorating dolls. She began selling her craftwork at the Lafayette Powwows. She found some members there willing to help her improve her crafting skills.

It was after World War II that she started going to meetings at the American Indian Federation in Lafayette, Rhode Island. Winona said that the Powwow was fully closed during the war. However, I remember Nashaweena telling me that the group always had a semi-Powwow or some sort of a celebration at least, on the Powwow dates. The organization was much more than a one day event.

Winona said that the Mohawks did not originally come to Lafayette when it was started in 1931. The original Powwows in the first few years consisted of a little bit of dancing, and usually a feast. The music was dependent upon whichever members attended and whatever talents they brought with them. It was a few years later when the Mohawk people came up from the Brooklyn, New York area and participated actively. These Mohawk people included Johnny Diabo, Louie and Louise Deer down from Caughnawaga, Canada, and Ben Massey, a Navajo.

I believe I first met Winona when we joined the American Indian Federation. She was active at that time and attended all of the meetings with her sister, Winifred. She participated in the dancing and sold her crafts at the annual Powwow. Her set ups were typical of all of the vendors at that time, usually a couple of rickety old card tables and a couple of old cotton "Indian" blankets sold at the local department stores. Today these blankets are treasured as collectibles.

In looking through my photo albums, I have found many

pictures circa 1940/1950 of Winona at Native activities and gatherings on Cape Cod. It appears that she was active in several areas during those years.

Winona was hospitable and welcoming to us. At the beginning of our involvement in Native activities she took me to the Cape and introduced me to Princess Evening Star (Gertrude Aiken) and her husband. For many years, they had programs in their backyard which was a beautiful grassy area with a natural amphitheatre. They invited dancers from all over the area to come for a weekend and perform for the public.

Princess Evening Star had a small Indian store near the side of the road from which she sold local crafts and Indian souvenirs. I am not sure how many years they had been putting on these programs. Unfortunately, we were never able to attend any of these programs, but how nice it must have been to see people come in and perform! We found out many years later that our friends Red Dawn (Stephen S. Jones, Jr.), who was an adopted Sioux and Blue Eagle, had been regular visitors to this program. We met them many years later when they were permanently performing at Fun Spot at Weirs Beach in New Hampshire.

Princess Winona's daughter, June Little Winona (June Hendrickson) left New England in 1966 to live in California to work and to be with her father. June was very active with her mother in her teen age and early adult years and she knows many of the people who immediately preceded the Bullock membership in the Lafayette group.

Winona never drove, so she had to rely on other people to get her to Powwows and Indian events. This did not slow her down, however. Carol Klein Moreau, who graduated from high school with June, did much of the driving in the early days. When we first met Winona, her sister Winifred, who had a car and drove, traveled with her extensively. As Winifred became less active, Winona made the acquaintance of a young lady, Coon Kitten (Louise Hebert). Louise is of Huron descent. At the time, Louise was single and very interested in participating in the Powwow circuit. She was an excellent driver, loved to travel, and had a pick-up truck which was in constant use. This enabled them to attend Powwows in the New England area. At other times, the Bullock family or Don Brennan transported Winona to and from Powwows with all of her trade goods, camping equipment, and her Indian outfits.

There was also a period of time when Winona owned her own station wagon. She had a series of friends who would drive this car to Powwows, thereby providing Winona with transportation and providing the driver with access to the Powwow and a wonderful weekend of fun and culture. Winona would have the station wagon all loaded up on Friday evening and off they would go to another adventure.

Princess Winona and Princess Nashaweena had always been very competitive and their sometimes difficult relationship was not going smoothly at this time. As I look back on it I feel that Nashaweena wanted members of the Indian Federation to be active within the organization but did not feel that members should be active in other Native organizations. She did not always encourage our participation in other Powwows. By this time, Princess Nashaweena had "been there done that." She was comfortable as the Squaw Sachem and I think that she resented our ability to travel further afield than she was able to.

We were very solicitous of Princess Nashaweena and took

her to other events which she enjoyed once she got there. But as she got older, it became more and more of a chore for her. Princess Winona was so outgoing and so active, getting to many different events; I think this contributed to the strained relations between the two women. Woe to the hapless fellow who mistook one for the other, calling one by the other's name!

Winona also brought me to Mashpee to attend a meeting of the Mashpee Wampanoag and there I met many people who became long-time friends: Princess Necia and her husband Broken Arrow, Big Toe, Smiling One, and Slow Turtle (John Peters). On the way back to Worcester from Mashpee that Saturday evening she asked if I would like to see some Indian dancing. Although Winona did not drive, she had a perfect sense of direction. She led us off into the woods, in what I later learned was the town of Wilkinsonville. We left Route 146 and meandered down an unfamiliar road and up a driveway, which went almost straight up to the clouds, past a house, and brought us down into the huge back yard.

There must have been 200 people. There were tipis set up, a dance circle with 50 or more dancers and Indian traders. As it was evening, they had a few lights and a blazing fire. This was my introduction to the American Indianist Society. We had no idea that such an event was held in New England, let alone within 30 miles of our home. She introduced me to some of the principals. It was there that we first met Sam One Bull, (Paul Fadden) who has remained a good friend of ours. We also met Ron Head and Jack Diegnan, who as youngsters were in the Swede Harrington Dance Team 20 years earlier. I had been a member of that dance team, too. Their interest had survived and lasted all that time. They had put their efforts and talents into this organization, which was so strong.

We stayed for a couple of hours. I remember that our son Chris had his tape recorder with him and he stood near the singers. The tape from that night still survives. This was probably the first time that our children had experienced a full scale Powwow, complete with both Northern and Southern music. This was a departure for us for we were accustomed to Eastern type music. This was something new to them and I think that the memory of that night will stay with them for the rest of their lives.

Princess Nashaweena was still active on the Indian scene even if she was slowing down a bit. She had received an invitation from the people at the Slater Mill complex in the center of the city of Pawtucket, Rhode Island, asking if she would put on an Indian program for one of their celebrations. Princess Nashaweena turned it over to us, and Princess Winona and I invited a number of dancers to participate. We probably had seven or eight dancers. Paul Fadden provided the music. The Slater Mill people provided very little advertising but the Powwow was significant in that we learned that we could indeed put on a very viable program, that the public was interested in events such as this, and that we thoroughly enjoyed participating.

To give you an idea of the scale of this, I think that they paid us so that we were able to provide for $3.00 gas money for each automobile that we needed to get us to the program. We were very excited about this and this was indeed the beginning of a whole lifetime of weekend Powwows and various events – just a thrilling way to spend our lives and an excellent way to help our children develop respect for others.

Over the next 25 years or so, Winona and the Bullocks attended many of the same Powwows, sponsored many

Powwows and always supported each other with our events. Although we were not partners in any sense of the word - we operated very independently - when it was a Powwow that Winona was attending we were there to support her and of course, she was always a part of our Powwows.

We were invited to participate at a Ceramic Show, which was held at Pawtuxet, Rhode Island. This was a convention of people who enjoyed the hobby of ceramic making and they had a trade show for people who wished to buy the crafts, molds and other raw materials, as well as finished products. The public was invited and it was well attended and I am sure that ceramic-related products sold very well. However, we found that American Indian related products were not on their wish lists. We sat through four long, long days behind our table watching people go by. Winona stayed at our house for those nights. Later, we were always able to communicate – tell each other whether a Powwow was going well or if business was a bit slow. All we had to say was "Ceramic Show" and we both knew what was happening or more to the point, not happening.

Princess Winona was known for her knowledge of Indian sign language. At Powwows, she would come up to the microphone and I would read the months of the year and then tell what they were called by the Indians (for instance, December was the dark moon) and she would do the moons in sign language. Nothing aggravated her more than to find that I did not have the listing and it was necessary for her to write them down again for me. It got so that I kept the listing in my wallet so that it was always available when called for. I carried that in my wallet for a year or so after Winona crossed. It was one of those items I carried in my wallet, like my license, credit cards and that sort of thing.

When we met Princess Winona she had already formed an organization in Worcester called the Indian Cultural Art Lodge. This was a very informal organization. The chief was Swift Hawk (Fred Mathews) and Sam One Bull was treasurer. The meetings were held every Friday night in Worcester at Winona's apartment. She owned a three decker and lived on the first floor. There were six or seven rooms which were completely filled with furniture, aquariums, Indian crafts, beading tables and comfortable rocking chairs and this became our Friday night home. I would get ready when I got home from work on Friday and sometimes Harriett would come with me but some of the kids always joined me. We would drive to Worcester, which is about 60 miles or so from home, to go to bead class. Winona taught everyone all types of beading: loom beading, rosette making, and daisy chain making. She would make her own moccasins. Sometimes we had a speaker or saw a film, but mostly we discussed crafts, language or attendance at upcoming Powwows. Everyone brought food to share. A short business meeting was held, and it was always very, very short because we were primarily interested in crafts and conversation.

One of the benefits of this relationship to our children was the intergenerational aspect. They learned to know older adults and to enjoy and respect others. True to the Native culture Elders are revered and respected. It is very important for children to be exposed to people of all ages. The kids loved to be there. This was part of our Friday entertainment, our education, and our Friday life. Sometimes when it got very late, one or two of the kids would fall asleep on the couch until it was time to go home. We seldom left before 11:00 in the evening; most of the time it was later than that. The ritual was to stop at Harry's Restaurant on Route 9 in Westborough, which was an all night restaurant - this was really part of the Friday night session. I think that frequently the kids came along because they also liked the special treat at Harry's on the way home.

The Cultural Art Lodge lasted for about 15 years. We couldn't go every Friday and of course, not everybody else could either. Everyone would go when they could - sometimes there would only be three of us and sometimes there would be 15 or 20.

Putting things into perspective can be a real eye opener. An example of this was a chance meeting I had with an Attleboro acquaintance who had sadly sent his son off to a distant college. This gentleman bemoaned being unable to see his son for two months until Thanksgiving vacation, due to the extreme distance. It turned out the son in question had traveled ALL the way to Worcester to college – such a long distance from home. This gentleman was somewhat taken aback upon learning that we drove to Worcester almost weekly!

When the holidays rolled around, the Lodge had a Christmas party. Somebody would bring a drum and we would do Round Dancing and Stomp Dancing throughout the house. The aquariums would shake and the windows would rattle and the music could be heard all over the neighborhood. Members brought special foods to share. Everyone brought their families – wives, husbands and children - it was a good family event. It became an annual, happily anticipated Christmas affair. After a few years Winona had an opportunity to go to California just before Christmas to spend the holidays with June. We decided to have the party after Winona returned; consequently our Christmas party was held in late January or early February for a number of years. When for various reasons, the celebration got later and later in the year, we felt that it would look a little odd to hold a Christmas party in the spring. We changed the name to Friendship Party.

The Friendship Party would include other people, not just the members of the Lodge and their families. The Friendship Parties continued to grow to the point that it became necessary for us to hire a private hall or a private room in a restaurant. These parties continued to grow for about another 10 years, until about a year before Princess Winona crossed over in 2003. These parties were always very spirited events. The food was the highlight and we always had an opportunity to do some dancing afterward. All of our friends would be there and it just became a very exciting informal event. This was probably one of the first socials to be held in the Indian community. The social is really the backbone of the New England Native community. Winona's Friendship Parties probably started the whole thing.

These social events were always sponsored by the Lodge. Refreshment, food, and expenses were covered by the treasury. The Lodge was not wealthy, but the members felt that sociability was important to foster and maintain in the Native community. All of the members pitched in and helped with donations of food, desserts and so forth. It was exciting to be able to participate.

Herb Johnson, who was a member of the Lodge, was instrumental in securing the use of a private campground in Sterling, Massachusetts (Pratt Junction). The Cultural Art Lodge sponsored a Powwow every Father's Day at that location until Winona passed away. The Powwows were self-supporting in that a small donation/admission charge was assessed to the general public. A little later on it was necessary to charge the traders a slight fee for camping. The cost of the campground was very minimal. The owner was most solicitous but he did incur expenses, which had to be paid. As the expenses increased over the years it was necessary that the rental fee also increase.

There was a very festive air to these Powwows. Actually, very little dancing was done. They were social events. The feast was held on Saturday evening and this was also paid for by the Cultural Art Lodge. Volunteers prepared the meal. I know that all of our boys, Andy, Chris, Dan and Ed helped prepare the feast for a number of years. Other volunteers also helped - Kevin Lantagne, Theresa & Bob Crowley and Gary Krofta. Don Brennan, Paul Fadden and Lee Crowley were also active in this capacity. Although I was not always able to attend these Powwows, I did go occasionally to help with the feast.

Four Moons (Don Brennan), as Chief, was very active in the Cultural Art Lodge and he was a most enthusiastic supporter of Winona's Powwow. He was always ready to lend a hand, to perform duties of Master of Ceremonies and to help Winona and June Little Winona with many of the necessary tasks.

This beautiful campground was a little bit off the beaten path and the advertising did not always click. Some years there would be a larger audience than others, but always there was a good Indian representation. It was a relaxing camping weekend and even if the traders did not sell very much, they all set up in an effort to support Winona. It was a huge field and its perimeter would be filled with all of the traders who were on the local circuit.

Winona had definite ideas on how a Powwow should be

run. She would call a planning meeting of the Lodge and once we were all assembled, she proceeded to tell us all of the plans and arrangements she had already made. When June Little Winona came back from California, she was Winona's right hand in the planning and execution of all that needed to be done.

Don Brennan as Master of Ceremonies

Drum groups would volunteer enthusiastically and there were a number of small dance programs held throughout both days. If the weather was hot, it could be that most of the dancers were swimming. The program would be held a little bit later when it cooled off. Winona's Powwows, like Winona herself, will be remembered for many years for the enthusiasm and for the spirit.

Perhaps here it would be appropriate to comment on "Winona the Camper." For many years, Winona had a 9x9 umbrella tent. She could pack this tent full of food, bedding, cots, trade goods, clothing, Indian outfits and tray tables. At this time she also traveled with her beloved dog, White Paw. Winona always came well prepared. If you needed anything, she had it either in her tent or her pocketbook, which must have weighed 15 pounds. I don't know how she managed to carry that pocketbook!

There is an interesting story about a Powwow held by the American Indianist Society in Rutland, Massachusetts. The Powwow was held on a field in the center of town. Around the perimeter of the field, a number of tipis, tents, and canopies had been set up. The benches were in place; the arbor had been constructed. Throughout the Powwow circuit Rutland was famous for rain. Sure enough, Saturday and Saturday night rains came down and the winds blew. The dance had to be held across the street in the gym of an elementary school. While we were dancing, the rain came harder and the winds started to blow fiercely. When the dance was over, all of the tipis and all of the canopies had blown over and only one tent was left standing - this was Winona's umbrella tent. I am sure the reason it was standing was that there was so much in it, the tent was too heavy to blow over.

In 1978, we made plans to attend National Powwow in Springfield, Missouri. At the time I had a new (to me) van. I took the third seat out and constructed five tables, three of which I could set up in the back of the van. We placed all of our bedding on the tables and all of our trade goods and clothing underneath the tables. We had three boys in the back seat (George Brousseau, Ed Bullock and one other boy) and Princess Winona rode in the front seat. I was the driver. Winona handled the maps - she was a great navigator. The further west we traveled, the more toll roads we encountered and Winona paid all of the tolls. She had her umbrella tent, of course, for her comfort. The boys and I slept in the van. We traveled through Ohio, visited museums, and went into the many huge caves in the area. We visited the museum under the arch in St Louis. When we arrived at the Powwow, Winona set up her tent, did the cooking and attended all of the activities. One of the days, we drove to the airport to meet June Little Winona, who had flown in from California to attend the Powwow and spend part of her vacation with us in Missouri.

Winona danced even into her mid 80's. In the tradition of the old Eastern Powwows, she not only was well known for her command of the sign language but she also danced a Blanket Dance. This is not to be confused with the Fancy Shawl Dance we see today, but rather was a dance performed by a woman with a blanket telling the story of a young Indian maiden who has not yet met her future husband.

The dance had been done for many years but I think Winona was the last one doing it on the circuit. She was always ready and willing to teach any enthusiastic dancer and she was very insistent that any young woman, who did this dance, did it correctly. If they could not, she would let them know that the dance steps and routine were not correct and it should not be done until it could be done the right way.

Princess Winona crossed over on January 28, 2003. She had always been active, always on the go, day or night. When asked to go anywhere, anytime, her answer was always "yes." She attended Powwows, did everything that she had always done, slowed down perhaps on her dancing a bit, but was still a main figure at every Powwow. She was active until about six days prior to her passing. She was in the hospital, and was kept comfortable. We all felt that she was aware of what was going on. Many of us were fortunate to see her at this time. When she died peacefully the 20-30 people assembled at the hospital very quietly sang her favorite song, "You Are My Sunshine."

A memorial planting of three young birch trees was held at the Rutland Powwow in the Rutland State Forest in 2004. Everyone was assembled, a few appropriate words were said, and the Walking Bear Singers, without the drum, sang "You Are My Sunshine." There was not a dry eye to be seen.

Princess Winona in some of her finery – Note her wonderful smile

As a further offering of respect to this amazing woman the following item was published in the Bullhorn, the newsletter of The Wandering Bull, Inc.

> *"They came from far and wide – from all the New England states from New York and even California – to pay tribute and to honor a giant of a woman, who had touched their lives. They came to pay respects to the family she so dearly loved. The snowy streets of Worcester had never experienced such an outpouring of love and loss. Her family stood by her as they had throughout her life and graciously shared with each of us some little part of this fine woman's life and love. Here was the epitome of the Native experience, the teacher, who was eager to share her knowledge and of course, her love. Each mourned but more than that they shared their stories and their love. Hers was an amazing life filled with peoples of all ages, with love and laughter and with fierce determination to share her knowledge and culture. Whether you called her Mother, Grandmother, Winona, or Auntie Jo you will miss Princess Winona. Perhaps we can honor her by continuing her mission of sharing and love, and by remembering that very special lady from Worcester who has taught us much. We thank her family for sharing this treasure of a woman with us. We are all richer for having known her."*

PRINCESS NECIA HOPKINS

I can't recall exactly when we met Princess Necia and Chief Broken Arrow (George Hopkins) but in the late 1960's they were a very integral part of the Powwow circuit, and became very much a part of the fabric of our lives. Princess Necia was a Schaghticoke and was Secretary of the New England Coastal Schaghticoke Association. Chief Broken Arrow, a Narragansett, later became Supreme Sachem of that tribe. The Chief of the New England Coastal Schaghticoke was John Farrar.

Princess Necia and Chief Broken Arrow were very friendly with Chief One Bear and Margaret Tremblay. The four of them traveled the Powwow circuit together.

During our early years with Princess Necia and Chief Broken Arrow, our children were very young, eager and impressionable. They looked up to all of the adults on the Powwow circuit as role models. Necia and George were most kind and thoughtful, going out of their way to offer encouragement and foster in them a deep love of the Native Culture.

At this time our boys did a lot of singing at local affairs with the "family" bass drum, although they were primarily dancers and enjoyed dancing more than singing. As they grew up, they became very proficient dancers and their outfits, which they made for the most part by themselves or by helping one another, became outstanding. They were fortunate enough to be invited to sing at Princess Necia's powwows.

A Powwow required music, and the boys were willing and able to supply quality singing. Although they may have started an event singing together, other people would frequently join them to round out the singing. It was entirely a "pickup drum" in those days. There were a number of singers who would join a pickup drum for a program. One of them was a fellow named Dan Pion who was a singer. Blackie Garabian (who later was instrumental in forming the Roaming Buffalo drum) always carried a drumstick in his back pocket and Scott Johnson from Sterling, Massachusetts often joined in the singing. Of course, all of the Powwows in the New England area were pleased when War Arrow (Steve Sando) and Joe Star came to sing. They could carry a Powwow program all by themselves, but other singers would frequently join with them. Wild Cat (Paul Cloud-Caruolo) attended many of the same Powwows and would occasionally sing, even though he preferred to dance.

Princess Necia seemed to be the Coordinator/Mistress of Ceremonies for an old traditional backyard type Powwow held on Route 138 in Easton, Massachusetts although I think the main sponsors were Chief Red Blanket and Lightning Foot (Cliff Wixson).. Princess Necia, at one point in her role as Mistress of Ceremonies, introduced the boys and me as "Whirling Thunder and the Thunderettes." Needless to say, the boys were not at all happy at being called the "Thunderettes" and every Powwow we attended after that where Princess Necia was at the microphone, the boys made me promise that they would not be called "Thunderettes."

Princess Necia and Chief Broken Arrow sponsored many Indian Powwows and programs. For many years, they held an indoor Powwow in late April/early May in a small church hall in Randolph, Massachusetts. When they outgrew the hall in Randolph, they moved to a church in Avon, Massachusetts, just down the road.

These Powwows were presented on a very small stage. By the time we got all the dancers, the singers and the drum on the stage along with the Master or Mistress of Ceremonies, there was very little space for dancing. We had to be careful that we did not collide with another dancer or that we did not fall off the stage. The stage was merely a wooden platform and the flooring vibrated so badly that we were always in fear of plunging through.

These programs were very popular and we enjoyed seeing people who regularly attended. During the program, we filed off the stage and danced up and down the aisles for the entertainment of the spectators. This event attracted many dancers and many Native people from the New England area. Being early in the Powwow season, people were eager to dance and to renew friendships even though it was an indoor event.

These were one-day events (Saturday). Necia and Broken Arrow cooked and prepared refreshments for sale and solicited home-baked items for desserts. These events, I believe, were quite successful for them and the gathering became an annual spring event.

After the Powwow, we were all invited back to the Hopkins' home in Randolph for a potluck feast. Necia supplemented the feast with all sorts of delicious home cooked items. We had so many people in this little house that I am sure the walls shook and certainly the floors felt the pressure of so many people dancing, talking and eating. To top off the festivities, a young lady named Leonda of the Cherokees shared her talent by singing and playing the guitar. The last we knew, Leonda was pastor of a small church on the Mohawk Trail.

One year we had so many appliances plugged in that George and I spent part of the evening in his cellar with a flashlight, replacing blown fuses. This did not deter the merry makers and a good time was had by all.

In addition to the springtime event, Princess Necia and Chief Broken Arrow also sponsored an August Powwow on the Mohawk Trail in Charlemont, Massachusetts. They knew Mr. and Mrs. Roberts, owners of an Indian Trading Post. An adjacent parcel of land was ideal for the Powwow. For many years, Princess Necia and Broken Arrow sponsored both the early spring and the August events.

Later on, when the church in Avon, Massachusetts was no longer available to them, they negotiated with Mr. and Mrs. Roberts and sponsored two Powwows per year in Charlemont, Massachusetts - one in early May and the other in August. The climate had not changed as much as it would in later years, so it was still apt to be cold, chilly, and damp for the early Powwow, but both events became very popular and went on for many years.

Princess Necia and Broken Arrow would go to the Mohawk trail a few days before the Powwow to set up the grounds. They purchased a large quantity of snow fencing which was installed around the field so that spectators had to come through the main entrance, thereby paying the entrance fee. There was a little restaurant on the far end of the Powwow grounds and if we wanted to go to the restaurant from our trader's space, we had to walk all the way to the main entrance and then double back to the restaurant and then back again. It became a sport for us to unroll George's fence so that we could go in and out without making the extra trip. George would come storming down the field to ask what happened to his fence. We would all appear very innocent. George would proceed to get his sledge hammer, replace the poles, unroll the fence and set up his fence line again. This was a bit of harmless fun to entertain us during the weekend.

The Powwow of course, was at the mercy of the weather. Even though we were there for the weekend, most would not don dance clothes and venture into the circle if it rained. We tried to put on a program but it was not always possible if the weather was inclement.

Princess Necia in a serious moment

One year, it rained all Friday evening and continued into Saturday morning. The field was wet, the grass was soggy and it continued to rain. We do not dance in the rain because it ruins not only our moccasins, but is detrimental to our outfits, our feathers, and our dispositions. Also, the singers are not able to go out in the rain to perform either, as moisture softens the head of the drum. The drum becomes flat and it is impossible to maintain the rhythm.

The gate however, was open and the tourists were coming through the entrance in hopes that some of the vendors would be open and that they would be able to see some of the dancing. They had paid their admission and Princess Necia felt that we should have some sort of a program for these people. She went from vendor to vendor asking people if they would come out and dance in the rain. Everyone said that perhaps they would dance in their jeans or shorts, but certainly we would not put on outfits or feathers.

Her next challenge was to get singers and there was no way the singers would bring the drum into the circle and face ruining the head of the drum. So, she went to her camp, got into her brown leather Indian dress, put on a pair of ankle high overshoes and an old red felt hat. This was shaped like a man's hat and the brightest red you had ever seen. She looked through the kitchen utensils in her camper and selected a very large aluminum soup pot and a large wooden spoon. Into the circle she went, introduced the program and proceeded to beat on the pan and sing in hopes that the rest of us would come into the circle and dance. Since we admired her spirit, some of us got into the circle and danced a little bit – putting on a very short program. Necia felt that the public had received their money's worth. We took the rest of the day off and the weather was better on Sunday.

These Powwow grounds in Charlemont were perfect in every sense of the word. There was a large level grassy area for the dance circle and all the traders, with a slight hill in the back topped by a level area. Participants set up their lodges, campers, and trailers on top of that hill. In addition to these amenities, there was a beautiful river directly across the street. This made the August Powwow particularly popular. It was most relaxing to walk across Route 2 and take a cool dip in the river that flowed slowly by.

Even though these Powwows evolved and changed over the years, it was still a very common practice to offer specialty dances. Many spectators attended year after year yet the specialties were always received very enthusiastically. Those dances made certain individuals popular. Princess Necia did a version of the Corn Dance where she would dance around the perimeter of the circle with a basket of corn kernels. The narrator of the dance told the story of the importance of corn to the Natives, both culturally and as food.

Chief Broken Arrow

Chief Broken Arrow, although he experienced trouble with his legs, always complied with a request for his Hunter's Dance. This was a dance telling (in pantomime) the story of a young brave out on the hunt trapping a deer. He would go through the motions of a warrior hunting, stopping by a stream, clearing the leaves from the water, placing his hands down in the water and bringing water to his mouth, point to the tracks he would see in the grass, move through the brush, finally spotting a deer, getting down on his knees, withdrawing the arrow from his quiver, placing the arrow in the bow, shooting the deer, then honoring the spirit of the deer. Then he would show the skinning of the animal, tying up the meat and slinging it over his shoulder and returning it to the village so that all the people could eat.

It is fitting here to note that in October 2011 at the York

Beach, Maine Powwow, White Horse (Ken Hamilton) paid homage to Chief Broken Arrow by performing the Hunter's Dance in the old traditional way. The circle of life continues with honor paid by today's young braves to Elders now crossed over.

Princess Necia also had a memorial greeting which she used at the beginning of the Powwow. She would announce herself as the "Teller of Tales" in a very loud voice and go on to list the people who had crossed over since the Powwow the previous year. A Powwow was a form of the Indian Telegraph; sometimes we called it the Moccasin Telegraph. As we came together from great geographic distances, we used the Powwow as an opportunity to update ourselves on friends and relatives. Today, email makes it much easier to keep informed, but we still pause at Powwows to remember those who have crossed over since our last meeting. We sometimes chuckled when Necia was going through her narration because we had heard it so often. I realize now how important that list was to us.

George and Necia conducted these Powwows in Charlemont for many years, until they retired. A MicMac friend of ours, Little Bear (Ray Larouche) took over the event for a while, running it very successfully. Gentle Moose (Paul White) and Peter Silva were among the Nipmuck people who supported this event. There were also a fairly large number of Wampanoag people who journeyed up from Southeastern Massachusetts to participate. This support helped to keep the event viable. Now the management has changed, but the Powwow continues on the same grounds. While we fondly remember our times at Charlemont, we have been unable to attend in recent years.

In the late 1980's, we were invited to participate in the Whole World Celebration, which was being held at the Hynes Auditorium in Boston. George and Necia, a friend of hers, Red Fox, from Connecticut, and some other friends split the cost of a large selling booth. The auditorium was huge and there were probably 200 or more booths set up - each one represented a different country or culture. We represented the American Indians, selling crafts and appropriate souvenirs and providing a dance program.

There was also a huge theater or hall with a large professional stage. Visitors could go into the theater at any time and see a short program provided by the representatives of the various countries and cultures. These multicultural segments lasted twenty minutes with a ten minute break in between. This break enabled the performing group to exit the stage and the next group to set up for their performance. It provided for a smooth transition but was not always easy for the performers, since they were given only a half hour's notice prior to the time they were required to be on stage. Meanwhile, we would have to scramble to get our outfits on and assemble the singers, dancers and drum. We would do a twenty minute program, leaving the stage promptly so that the next group could put on its demonstration.

The whole celebration lasted four or five very long days. We left home early in the morning, worked all day, put on programs that lasted till 8:30 or 9 pm, drove home to Attleboro and then were expected to be back in the morning to start all over again. The daytime audience was comprised almost exclusively of students from middle and junior high schools. They were bused into Boston from every town and city in Massachusetts. The evening performances were family oriented and a little less hectic.

Broken Arrow was not enthusiastic about putting on programs or dancing for any length of time. The twenty minute segments pleased him immensely, but the rest of us felt that it never really gave us the opportunity to put on a quality program or to peak out. We find that programs where Indian music is involved should last a minimum of forty five minutes. It takes some warm-up time to have the music at its best, and the dancers need time to limber up. Generally speaking, singers and dancers enjoy what they do so much that once started, they are reluctant to stop – certainly not in 20 minutes! At best, it requires a male dancer at least 20-25 minutes to change from street clothes into full regalia. Women and girls can generally make the same change in much less time. This seems to be the reverse of most cultures.

Supreme Sachem George Broken Arrow Hopkins died in November 1996 at the age of 81 and Princess Necia died December 12, 2004 at the age of 84. Their contribution to our culture is huge – they are missed.

STAR AND CLEAR SKY

We met Star and Clear Sky shortly after we became active in the American Indian Federation. Our connection to this amazing Native couple and their family grew and blossomed as we became more involved in their programs and learned more about their Southwestern culture. They were always warm and welcoming. They patiently taught their dances and music and opened up a whole new world to us - this friendship was extremely important, especially to our children. Our relationship with this couple helped reinforce the values we were teaching our youngsters.

Clear Sky and Star

Star (Joe Colaque) was born on the Jemez Pueblo in New Mexico on September 2, 1917. Growing up, he spent time between Jemez and the Cochiti Pueblo which was a day's walk over the mountains or a long journey by wagon. Today, it is a relatively short trip by automobile on good roads. Joe spoke about the hike through the mountains with his sister – it was long and dangerous, but they were met with such warmth and love upon arrival that it was worth the trip. Joe remembered being brought up by a family on Cochiti and when we accompanied Joe to the Buffalo Dance at Cochiti, we all were treated with love and respect by this entire family.

Joe attended St. Catherine's boarding school and found it difficult to adjust to the structure and routine. He ran away around age 13 with another youngster who seemed to be more worldly than Joe. They traveled the rails all around the Mid West, fending for themselves as best they could. He joined the circus at one point and arrived in Chicago about the time the World's Fair was closing in 1933. There, he met other Native people, many of whom had participated in the World's Fair. This performance concept may have sparked an interest in him, which would be realized years later.

As World War II was starting, Selective Service was able to track Joe down, requesting he report to his draft board. He visited Jemez prior to entering the United States Army. This was his first visit back home in several years. His Army training took him to Fort Devens in Ayer, Massachusetts, where he gathered about 34 other Native young men and formed a dance team. A large order for regalia supplies was compiled and sent to Plume Trading & Sales Co. in New York City - coincidentally this was the same Plume Trading & Sales Co. which the Wandering Bull, Inc. purchased in 1986. The Army gave the group a large room to house their activities. They used the room for storage, craftwork and dance practice.

The room was the office of Bill Mauldin, a wartime artist who was also preparing to go overseas. Mauldin created two characters, G.I.'s Willie and Joe, whom he used during the war with brilliant and poignant humor to put smiles on the faces of the soldiers throughout some of the horrible war experiences that followed.

The Devens dance group performed in Massachusetts and southern New Hampshire, dancing wherever they could. It must have been a relief for these young men to participate in their traditional dances, while preparing to go overseas and fight for their country.

At this time Clear Sky, in her Native garb, was on a War Bond Drive with Sally Rand, a 1930's Fan Dancer. Clear Sky was noted telling Sally Rand that Sally got paid for taking her feathers off and Clear Sky got paid for putting her feathers on. In Boston, Massachusetts, Clear Sky and Joe Star met and joined forces, putting on Indian dance programs and selling War Bonds. These War Bond Drives had a huge response from the general public and many bonds were purchased.

Joe was a proud member of the 45th Thunderbird Division. Joe and his Division were sent to North Africa and then on to Italy. Joe spoke of walking his way through Europe while fighting for his country. He modestly and somewhat reluctantly told of his experiences during World War II. He was part of the liberating force at Dachau Prison Camp - a memory never to be forgotten. He made several life-long friends during this time. The agony and tragedy of war weighed heavily on him. This journey was two years of horror, but ultimately winning the war was a grim satisfaction to those G.I.'s who had given so much to their country.

Back in the States, Joe and Clear Sky reunited. Clear Sky's first husband, Karl Holt, had passed away. Star and Clear Sky settled in Beverly, Massachusetts, where Joe worked for the U.S. Post Office and Clear Sky maintained their home.

It was not long before they traveled to Jemez Pueblo and brought Joe's niece Esther back to Beverly to live with them. Esther had all of the benefits of living off reservation but was able to maintain her ties to Jemez and the Pueblo culture with frequent trips back to New Mexico. Under the name "Along the Moccasin Trail," this family danced and sang in the Pueblo style, opening up a new world to the New Englanders they encountered.

Esther completed high school in Beverly and went on to earn her Registered Nurse credentials at Beverly Hospital.

Esther married War Arrow (Steve Sando) who was also from Jemez. They settled in Beverly where they raised their three children, Morning Cloud (Karl), Snow Flower (Tina) and

Martin Star. Frequent visits to Jemez, and one trial move there, resulted in them finally relocating in New Mexico.

After we met this lovely and talented family, we were privileged to join them in a number of programs and they often provided music for our events. They invited us to participate in their program during the Topsfield Fair in the fall. This was done on one of the center stages on the grounds and was enjoyed by the many spectators attending the fair. It was pretty thrilling for our children to be on stage at such a large and diverse event. Of course, they had the Sando children to keep them busy in between the shows, which were scheduled throughout the weekend. We did this program for several years with Star and Clear Sky and family.

Red Deer (Billy Muniz) and his wife Barbara also participated in these programs at Topsfield. Red Deer was quite a crowd pleaser and enjoyed putting on a good performance for the audience. This was a time before cell phones and picture taking were as pervasive as today, but the spectators managed to take many photographs so that there would be a visual record of the event. Never to be out done, Red Deer on occasion would turn to the audience and

Red Deer

take out a camera, proceeding to reverse the action and take photos of them. This always got a laugh from the crowd.

In order to insure that the spectators at Topsfield Fair had a good Native performance to watch, Star and Clear Sky occasionally brought in other dancers to vary the program. One summer afternoon we were invited to a picnic at their home in Beverly where we met the Fletcher family, Fred and Carol and their children. Fred, like his father before him, was a bonnet maker and a "feather man." This family was a colorful addition to our small troupe.

Another time they had a contract with the Deerskin Trading Post which was located on Route 1 not too far from Beverly. This company was in the process of opening several new locations and the Star and Clear Sky family was contracted to perform at each location during its opening weekend. We danced at the Danvers location and in Pembroke, right off Route 3, for that opening.

The Saturday of the Pembroke opening weekend was extremely warm - well, really hot. Everybody danced their best in spite of the heat and their warm regalia. As things began to settle down after the program, a couple of spectators approached our group, and commented on the program and the heat. They went on to invite the entire group to their home on Boot Pond in nearby Plymouth. This was a wonderful opportunity to cool off and this charming couple, Jack and DeDe, were most gracious, even firing up the grill to feed everyone. We saw Jack and DeDe around the Powwow circuit for several years after that. I believe they had a business at that time called Boot Pond Feather Merchants. Meeting this gracious couple helped the children see how generous and giving people could be.

One of the features of the Pembroke opening was a traditional Plains tipi, complete with all the authentic furnishings. This was set up by Bob and Carole Moreau, who also were dancers and craftspeople. They carefully explained the significance of each item and answered questions. Although the Native people in this area did not live in tipis, this was a learning experience for both adults and children. Shortly after this weekend, Bob and Carole moved to the Southwest. Their knowledge and expertise would be sorely missed but they went with the best wishes and love from all who knew them.

Clear Sky, Wawedaki (Carl Bullock), and Joe Star - Carl's naming ceremony

Another location of Deerskin Trading Post was opened in Western Massachusetts, almost to the New York border. Of course, we were invited to participate in this opening as well. We piled the six kids into the VW bus and started the long trip along the Mass Turnpike. While Southeastern Massachusetts is relatively flat, Western Massachusetts is very hilly, and the VW bus did not do well on hills, especially when loaded with eight people, trade goods, regalia, camping supplies and food for the weekend. We putted along, encouraging the vehicle to do its best and finally arrived at our destination with precious little time to spare before Grand Entry. I think our friends knew that we were dependable, but they may have questioned our mode of transportation. Once again, it was a great weekend and we all had a wonderful time.

These traits of reliability and dependability were fostered in our children and the lessons were subtle but effective. They knew that the adults were people to be looked up to and admired.

The high point of each performance was the Hoop Dance by Joe Star. He executed this very complicated and taxing dance at each program. Even into his fifties, Joe did the Hoop Dance

Joe Star – the Hoop Dance

Rodney Brewer – Hoop Dance as taught by
Joe Star

to thunderous applause. True to the tradition of education and honoring his culture, Joe helped several young men master this dance, so that even today on the Powwow circuit we can enjoy "Joe Star's Hoop Dance" as performed by one of his protégés. What a thrill it is to see his talent live on in his students.

Shortly after Andy's high school graduation, he was invited

Karl Sando, Paul, and Joe Star in New Mexico, 2001

to spend a week with Star and Clear Sky, an invitation which he quickly accepted. The days were spent with Clear Sky and her friend Dottie Nunn, touring all of the attractions on the North Shore, while the evenings were spent learning silver-smithing from Joe. What kind and thoughtful people they were and how very much Andy gained from that experience. He proudly brought Harriett back a ring that he had made under Joe's tutelage.

As time passed, Steve and Esther and their family moved to Jemez a second time, this was to be a permanent move. This move deeply troubled Star and Clear Sky, who wanted their little family close together. Clear Sky crossed over on March 5, 1995 and was buried with her extended family in a little country cemetery in Raynham, Massachusetts.

Joe Star ultimately married an old friend, the widow of one

Clear Sky several years before she crossed over

of his World War II buddies, and relocated to Virginia. During Star's final months he was cared for by his family in Albuquerque. On our last visit it was heartwarming to see the respect, love, and devotion showered on him by the entire family, but especially by his grandsons. Joe Star crossed over on May 9, 2004 at his niece, Esther's home in Albuquerque. His final resting place is his beloved Jemez. Although his travels took him to many far off places, his birthplace Walatowa (Jemez Pueblo) remained in his heart forever. He never forgot its traditions, sacred ceremonies and the Towa language.

We think of these wonderful people often and know that they are dancing and teaching still.

LIMEROCK

In 1972, Ed McDermott, a member of the North Smithfield Historical Society in Rhode Island, coordinated a Powwow, which was held in Limerock, Rhode Island. Spotted Eagle was the Native American liaison between the Historical Society and the Indian community. The Powwow was held in late September of each year until about 1977.

The Powwow grounds were on the old Rhode Island Route 146, across from the building owned by the Historical Society. During the Powwow events, this building was open. The Society members sold light refreshments, and Spotted Eagle, who was quite an artist, displayed many of his paintings there.

The Powwow site was very uneven and rocky. The whole area was part of a hill. There was really only one portion that would accommodate a rather small grassy circle. At the top of the hill was a fence line and those campers who had come for the weekend, traveling from New York, New Jersey and Connecticut, would set up their tents there. The vendors would be near the bottom of the hill, along the side of the road. Today, this formerly pristine area has been developed into a residential neighborhood.

The Limerock Powwow was what I would call a "transitional Powwow." It was one of the last of the "backyard Powwows," which consisted of a single Master of Ceremonies who drummed and sang, providing all of the music. It was necessary for him to be able to vary the program by telling stories, explaining the customs, telling a little bit about the Indian language, and doing things to keep the audience interested. At the same time, he had to catch his breath so that he could sing the next song. At this particular time, Powwows began to change, making it difficult for one man to conduct the entire program himself. Northern drums replaced the single Master of Ceremonies and those people who could carry an entire program were replaced by a different style of music. Dancers were requesting more "intertribal" dances and music.

There were only a few people on the circuit at that time who could perform as Master of Ceremonies for the programs in this old style. The most well-known Masters of Ceremonies, whom I knew, were Strong Horse (Ken Smith), who was prominent at many of the New England Powwows, Onkwe Tase (Ed Guillemette), and of course Bright Canoe (John Diabo), a Mohawk gentleman who lived in Brooklyn, New York and participated in many of the programs in this area. Another New Yorker seen in this area was Green Rainbow (Louie Mofsie) who headed up the Thunderbird Dancers and provided a comprehensive program to the delight of the audience. Strong Horse (Ken Smith) was Master of Ceremonies at most of the Limerock Powwows.

We were beginning to hear different styles of music in the early 70's. Drum groups, using a large drum and more than one singer, singing Northern music, were becoming popular at this time. Four Moons (Don Brennan) remembers that Joe Star and War Arrow (Steve Sando) came for at least part of the program and sang their Northern style music. Although Joe Star and Steve Sando were Pueblo, they sang in the Northern style for general Powwow dancing. When they were performing traditional Pueblo dances, the music was traditional Pueblo as well.

This was one of the first times at a Powwow in Rhode Island that the Northern style drum group was utilized. Drum groups were becoming more popular in the New England area in

general, but I don't think that the Rhode Island Powwows were the first to switch over from a single singer to a drum group.

Don Brennan

The Limerock programs consisted primarily of specialty dances, including Hunter's Dance, Challenge Dance, and Welcome Dance. These were explained and narrated by the Master of Ceremonies. It was necessary for the Master of Ceremonies to be aware of who was in the dance circle and of their specialty dances. There were also intertribal dances, in which all Native people, young, old, men and women, and even children, got into the circle and danced. It was the task of the Master of Ceremonies to keep the Powwow organized and moving smoothly.

Many of the older people would participate by coming into the circle at Grand Entry and participating in a few of the dances. They would frequently take a turn at the microphone later in the program, introducing themselves or telling an interesting story to the spectators. In fact, all of the participants were expected to go to the microphone and introduce themselves, as well as indicate their tribal affiliation and current home town.

All of the Indians who came to a Powwow were expected to participate in the dance program. In order to do that, it was decided that the traders would not sell when the program was going on. Competition among traders was brisk at this time. Traders were expected to sell only Indian made goods and for the most part, they kept an eye on each other's wares to make sure that manufactured, imported, or other non-Indian made souvenirs were not offered for sale. For instance, a young woman selling commercially made crafts was asked to leave because the goods were not Indian made.

Our children loved to dance. Frequently, a single Master of Ceremonies who was trying to save his voice and his singing ability would have to spend a lot of time talking and entertaining. The kids became very impatient with this but were always well behaved in the circle. They were eager, ready, willing and able to step up and dance. A Powwow that offered enough music and a lot of dancing was right down their alley. This is what they lived for in a Powwow.

Some of the people who attended as performers and traders were One Bear (Raymond Tremblay) and his wife Little Fawn (Margaret), Broken Arrow (George Hopkins) and his wife Necia, Maise Shenandoah, and a family by the name of Brown. (I have lost track of the Browns over the years but I think they were Oneida.) Princess Winona, Tall Oak (John Neidijadlo) and his wife Margaret, Big Thunder (Fred Reynolds), Twin Skies (Louie Deer), his wife Green Leaf (Louise), Fleet Wing (Anne Chick) and her mother Ann also attended this Powwow. As mentioned before, the Joe Star family: Clear Sky, Steve War

Arrow, Esther Orange Blossom (Esther Sando), Karl, Tina and Star also brought their own music and dance style to these events.

Many people who attended Limerock did not generally participate in Powwows in the Rhode Island area. For example, a number of people from the Iroquois Nations set up regularly at this event. Maisie Shenandoah was one of those who participated every year. One year, she had her daughter, Joanne, with her. Maisie narrated, I think it was the Lord's Prayer, while Joanne acted it out in sign language. Little did we know that Joanne would go on to national fame as a singer of Native American music. Many of you probably have her recordings or have seen her in concert.

At this time I developed a fascination with the Oneida people and their packing ability. When the Powwow was over in the evening, they piled all of their things in a four foot square pyramid, wrapped it all up with canvas tarpaulin tied with a rope, and it would stay there through wind and rain, sleet and snow. I recognize the Oneidas as being the masters of packing.

Fleet Wing (Anne Chick), a member of Lafayette and of the Wollomonuppoag Indian Council, has crossed over, but as her legacy, she left a large collection of stone artifacts gathered by her family in the Wrentham, Massachusetts area over the years. This collection was willed to a man in that community who I believe was connected to the Police or Sheriff's Department. He contacted me asking if I knew of an organization which would accept this collection as a gift in memory of the Chick Family.

Welcome Dance at Limerock Powwow, 1974

Challenge Dance, 1974

At the time, I was a Trustee of the Robbins Museum in Middleboro and Dr. Curtiss Hoffman was the president. The Museum accepted this offer and the collection is still on display at the Museum. Because the origin of all these artifacts has not been documented, the collection, although valuable and accurate, lost considerable value as far as museum display was concerned. But it remains invaluable as a teaching tool. The museum, I believe, still uses these artifacts in some of their outreach educational programs.

Princess Nashaweena (Sadie Barry), who was beginning to slow down and not get around as much as she had earlier, was very interested in this Powwow but also very concerned about it. She felt that if too many Powwows were held in the area, it would dilute the success of some of the old traditional Powwows. Although she was reluctant to go, I was able to get her up there one year. She visited, talked with friends and when I brought her home early in the afternoon, I think she felt that it was a good Powwow. Since the Powwow was held late in September each year, and at that point it was late in the season, I don't think that it conflicted very seriously with any other activity being held in the area. Wouldn't she be surprised at the depth of today's Powwow schedule!

Eagle Feather (George Curtis), was a new friend and had attended the Limerock Powwow at our invitation. Harriett and I and some of the kids were at an ice cream stand in Norton, Massachusetts when a fellow came in and sat at the counter. Because of his dress and demeanor we thought he might be Native. We were a little shy about approaching him because we were uncertain, but he certainly appeared to be a Native gentleman. I guess we mustered up our courage and approached him and indeed, George Curtis was Native and a resident of Plainville, Massachusetts. He had been on the periphery of Indian activity for many years but had never been actively involved. We invited George to attend this Powwow due to its timing and proximity. He came, and over the years he became a very good friend of ours, became active, made an outfit and danced at many of the Powwows. Several years later, he was one of the leaders instrumental in helping Big Thunder (Fred Reynolds) organize the Wollomonuppoag Indian Council.

John Running Deer (John Eleazer) lived in New York and we met him at many Powwows from New Jersey/New York to Loon Mountain, New Hampshire. He attended the TOPIC Powwows and the Mashpee Powwow Fourth of July weekend. He always had a green sports car and his outfit was predominately green. I guess his favorite color was green. John Running Deer was a tremendous dancer and a good sport. We always enjoyed participating in Indian programs with him. He added a lot to whatever Powwow he attended. As there have been a number of John Running Deers on the Powwow circuit - several at the same time - it can be confusing.

GILBERT STUART BIRTHPLACE

In the late 1970's Princess Nashaweena was invited to put on a dance program at the Gilbert Stuart Birthplace in Saunderstown, Rhode Island. Gilbert Stuart was an artist in colonial times, who was well known for his brilliant paintings of George Washington and many of our founding fathers. His birthplace has been restored and is a privately owned non-profit entity.

Stuart's father had a grinding wheel operation utilizing a stream, which flowed through his property. As I remember it, the shoreline was beautiful and somewhat different than what we normally expect to see now along the New England Coast. The paths and the lawn were well cared for and the lawn area went right down to the water. There were coves and small peninsulas along the coastline. It was a most relaxing and peaceful section of Rhode Island. Today it still maintains its character, is open to the public and is maintained by the caretakers, who live in the restored home on the grounds.

Princess Nashanweena knew the people who were caretakers at that time and she was invited on numerous occasions to put on a small program with a reception for the public in a beautiful shaded glen adjacent to the mill. We were invited to put on a dance program and we had with us a small group of Boy Scouts who at that time, were working on the Indian Lore Merit Badge. We decided that we would do something a little different so we had our participants go through the woods to a spot out of sight of the grounds. We brought our own canoes and also borrowed additional watercraft from the caretakers. It was a beautiful sunny day and our singers started the program with a Calling Song. As the song progressed we paddled the canoes to a site very close to the mill. It made quite an impression to see the people in regalia arriving at the Powwow via canoe. It was a very successful program and we all had a lot of fun. The only mishap was when Chief Broken Arrow tripped getting out of the canoe and fell overboard.

We put on a small program which was well received. Senator and Mrs. Claiborne Pell were invited guests and were most gracious. This was one of the first times that the Bullock

Family had set up a "trading table." We had been selling our Native American note paper and we also had a line of 9 or 10 different Native American embroidered patches, which we secured from a gentleman in the Chicago area.

I remember that Harriett received a couple of orders for ribbon shirts. She had been making them for quite some time for family members and friends. This represented some of her first sales to the general public.

We had ample time for singing and dancing. The Native People and the Boy Scouts had a great deal of fun with the singing, dancing, and entertaining. Following the afternoon program the host prepared a delicious buffet which was set up underneath the grape arbor. It did not take long for the Natives and the Boy Scouts to avail themselves of the many delicacies. Princess Nashaweena was invited into our hosts' home and was served her meal there. The rest of us had finished eating, changed out of our regalia and were ready to leave but waited for Nashaweena to finish. We, of course, provided transportation for her and we would not leave until she was ready. This was the traditional way and although all of the participants were ready to leave, everyone was happy to wait until Princess Nashaweena was ready.

Princess Nashaweena was always eager to put on a program and was a superb Mistress of Ceremonies. I believe that is the only time that we did the Gilbert Stuart Birthplace program but it remains a very happy memory for the entire Bullock family.

POINTE BLEUE

In July of 1980 Bright Canoe invited us (the family) to attend the American Indian Festival in Pointe Bleue, Quebec. Pointe Bleue (now in 2013 called Mashteuiatsh) is the Montagnais Indian Reserve on Lac Saint Jean. We drove first to Caughnawaga Indian Reserve and stayed at Bright Canoe's home one night and then we followed Bright Canoe and his friend Albert on the drive the next day to Pointe Bleue, 228 miles north of Montreal.

The Montagnais are bush people. They hunt and trap for their livelihood. The adults leave the village in the fall and travel into the bush where they live in tents for the entire winter. These white tents are equipped with a stove and a chimney, that goes through a hole in the roof of the tent just as our chimney goes through a hole in the roof of our home. Now these tents are purchased from various sources throughout Canada and are all basically the same design. I understand that originally they were purchased from the Hudson's Bay Company.

The villagers spent the entire winter in the bush hunting, trapping, and preparing the furs for sale upon their return to the village in the spring. Of course, many years ago they would travel using sleds and dogs, but today skimobiles are much more popular.

Their travels would take them fifty to eighty miles into the bush. The men were generally accompanied by their wives on these trapping expeditions. The children would have to go to school, so they remained on the Reserve and lived in the school dormitory until the adults returned for the summer.

The school was closed in the summertime, so the committee housed our little dance group in one of the dormitories. We found it immaculately clean and we were able to utilize the gym for our dance practice sessions.

Our group consisted of seven people: Dan, Ed, Faith, Harriett, Albert, Paul, and Bright Canoe. Harriett did not dance but she provided support and advice for the entire festival, kept us all on schedule and helped us with our outfits.

The weeklong festival included many sports type competitions: foot races, swimming, canoe racing, rifle shooting, and bannock cooking. The most spectacular event for us to witness however, was the tumpline contest where the men would carry heavy loads in canvas bags by means of a strap around their heads. The object was to carry the most weight the furthest distance. It was fascinating to witness this event and we marveled at the strength displayed. Because these burdens weighed in excess of two hundred pounds, it was necessary that the pavement be cleaned before each contest so that the contestant would not slip or fall on even the smallest grain of sand. A slight misstep or slip would cause the person to do serious harm to his back or legs.

Montagnais people are very gentle and have a great sense of humor. They thoroughly enjoyed all of the daily events.

Over time, their language has become a combination of Montagnais and French and a translator is a must. Albert served as our translator. He spoke French and was somewhat familiar with the Montagnais language as well. We found it convenient to have Albert nearby, enabling us to properly answer questions and communicate. The only Reservation people we met who could speak English were the Catholic Priest at the local church and a tribal policeman who was originally from Caughnawaga.

We were there for three days, putting on three programs per day, which was a real working experience. Although the people could not understand what we were talking about, they were very enthusiastic about our dancing and would cheer, stomp their feet, and clap as we danced. They were very intrigued with our outfits, taking every opportunity to introduce themselves, ask about our clothing, and discuss our dancing.

We saw many people who had at least partial regalia. Unfortunately, over the years their songs and dances had been lost. They were most interested in regaining the knowledge, seeing the dances, and hearing the music. Some of the men wore a Western style headdress. Many of them had beautiful leggings (or pants) and leather shirts, which were decorated with beadwork or moose hair embroidery. The leather and furs were beautifully tanned and we also noticed a distinct leaning toward the use of Scottish plaids. The women had skirts made of the plaid and some wore hats tailored in a military style. We assume that the Montagnais were much influenced by the Scottish people.

Most of the activities took place along the lakefront. Although all of the contests attracted a lot of attention, it is not surprising that the food held its own in popularity. A block long barbeque had been constructed at lakeside with many rotating spits set up over the coals. Here, many game meats and local favorites were slow cooked. We enjoyed beaver, deer meat and moose meat. These were prepared in many different ways. We found one of our personal favorites to be a stew made of moose meat and deer meat along with numerous vegetables - very similar to our beef stew at home. We were invited to visit in a number of homes and enjoyed their sincere hospitality, their interest, and their cooking.

The homes on the Reserve are modern in every respect. The yards are well tended. I guess as a reluctance to surrender to modern living, many of these homes had a tent complete with stovepipe in their back yard. Families lived in these tents during the summer months even though they had a modern home nearby. It was not unusual to see pens in the back yards

Our group – Ed, Dan, Bright Canoe, Paul, Faith, Albert

housing some young wild animals which were treated very much as family pets.

This trip was one of our great family adventures. Our children enjoyed meeting all of these people. We found various ways of overcoming the language gap. Dan had had two years of high school French and was able to get us through when Albert was not available.

Bright Canoe was the Master of Ceremonies and always handled that task in a very professional manner. He did not however, speak either French or Montagnais, but he introduced each segment of the program and attempted to teach the audience how to count from one to ten in Mohawk. Because the audience did not speak either English or Mohawk, Albert stepped up to the microphone to translate Bright Canoe's words into French. Bright Canoe did enjoy talking and his descriptions were frequently very lengthy. We would chuckle each time Bright Canoe would take three or four minutes to introduce a dance and then Albert would translate the story in a ten second sound bite.

Although the lakefront was busy all week long, it was the Sunday Mass that attracted the largest crowd. The Mass was conducted on the stage, which had been constructed at the waterfront. Crowds of people of all ages stood on the pavement and the local priest conducted the Mass. It was most interesting. The altar was an upturned canoe supported by sawhorses and covered with the appropriate altar cloths and local greenery. At the Presentation of the Gifts, a young couple in Indian regalia presented a pair of snowshoes and a beaver pelt. A full choir dressed in Indian regalia - the men with Western style headdresses - was a highlight of this religious celebration.

Village men preparing for the contest

A dance session on the stage at Pointe Bleue

The Pointe Bleue Festival was the first opportunity that many of the people on the Reserve had to see their old friends since the previous fall. This event was so popular that it also attracted many people who had moved off the Reserve, and gave them an opportunity to participate in the reunion.

Albert, Dan, Ed, and Faith with some of the youngsters

The program was advertised and there were a number of tourists who came to see and participate. We met many people from various countries in Europe and many Canadians, primarily from the Montreal area. Tourists and outsiders were welcomed, but the emphasis of the entire festival was the opportunity for a reunion of the people of the Reserve. As our stay came to a close, we were very sad to leave these wonderfully warm people and there were many hugs and handshakes as we got into our van to return home.

I think of all of the wonderful experiences that we have enjoyed as a family, Harriett and I felt that our children were most impressed by the Montagnais people and experienced the same feeling of sadness as we left this beautiful Reserve.

Our trip from Montreal to Pointe Bleue had been quite direct. We were in a hurry to get to Pointe Bleue and had very little time to explore and sightsee on the way up. We were following Bright Canoe and Albert and found it a challenge to keep up with the lead car. They were driving a relatively new vehicle and we were in an older van. In addition to the five of us, we had all of our clothing and all of our outfits. We learned that Albert had a lead foot. I also had the feeling that the Quebec police might not be as understanding of our endeavors since we had a Massachusetts registration plate. However, as we returned home we were able to spend more time and had a very leisurely ride down through the Laurentian Mountains, which we had never seen before. It was a memorable ending to a very memorable trip.

To update the Pointe Bleue story a little bit, in 2005 at the Sturbridge Powwow, I was talking with Black Feather who is one of the very few Montagnais people I have met in the States. He has been away from Pointe Bleue a number of years, but keeps in contact with friends and relatives who still live there. We discussed the many changes since 1980 that have taken place on many of the Reserves. The technology age has brought computers, email and i-Pods to these people and they have become very worldly. It was comforting to know they have maintained their good nature and sense of humor. This was indicated by one of Black Feather's friends who had recently emailed him to say that the local hospital was most up to date and had recently been the recipient of a donation of a new dialysis machine. They had been assured that the electricity would be available within the year. This story renewed our memories of a delightful and noble people.

The celebration of Mass on Sunday morning
in Pointe Bleue

YORK BEACH POWWOW

After graduation from college in May 1988, our son, Ed Bullock decided that he would like to live in York Beach, Maine. Rather than go into the corporate world, it was his ambition to open a Native American store in York Beach. He named his new enterprise *the little bull,* which was a slight take on The Wandering Bull. His first store was in one room adjacent to the Paras Pizza restaurant. The first year was a successful adventure. He was able to rent a larger store three or four buildings closer to the ocean for the second year.

As of this writing, Ed has had the store for 25 years and it has thrived, featuring Native American made crafts - pottery, kachinas, headdresses, sterling & turquoise jewelry, and other related products. This has become a very successful seasonal business (May through October). Ed has developed a large customer following. People from all over the East Coast find their way to *the little bull.*

York Beach is a very popular vacation spot. Families who originally built cottages or homes in the community have established a semi-permanent residence and children, grandchildren and great grandchildren continue to summer there.

York Beach Powwow came about in 1989 when Mrs. Verna Rundlette approached Ed and asked him to present an Indian program in conjunction with the annual summer event "York Beach Days." We discussed this at great length and decided that it would be a lot of fun. We didn't realize that it would become an eleven year tradition in York Beach. While it was a labor of love, it required many months of preparation time and hard work.

It was our wish that every year would be better than the year before. It was not a case of being bigger, but of being better. We succeeded in doing just that. The quality of the Powwow presentation was better each year, so of necessity, it became bigger. The first year we presented the program on the ball field, which was adjacent to the York tourist area and the beach itself. A portion of the field was set aside for Ed's Powwow activities. The "York Beach Days" committee was very kind and generous, especially supplying appropriate publicity for the event.

A parade was held in conjunction with York Days and we were invited to participate. Ed was able to borrow a flat bed truck (with a driver). We decorated it with Native American-related articles and a great many bales of straw - also borrowed. We had a large drum on the flat bed with three or four singers to provide music. A number of Native people in regalia were seated on the straw bales which made it possible for many of our Elders and very young people to participate in the parade. Whenever the parade paused, the singers provided music and the rest of us danced in the street, much to the delight of the spectators. The parade organizers provided a number of trophies in various categories. The Native American float received a first place trophy for "Best in Parade."

The weather was perfect and our program attracted a great many spectators. Verna also asked if we would put on an evening program at the beach itself, utilizing the covered pavilion for the singing groups. Many of our participants had traveled a great distance for a one-day event so this evening program presented problems for us. For one thing, it was a project to dismantle the speaker system and physically move it to the beach. Additionally, the dance area at this location was on a slight incline and the grass became slippery in the early evening. This made dancing difficult, so it was with a great deal of reluctance that we agreed to do this program. As it turned out, this became a delightful traditional event with many people attending. The program was so popular that the audience would not let us stop, so we danced well into the darkness of the evening.

Our first year, we found it difficult to locate dancers and craftspeople in the York Beach area. However, the southern New England Powwow circuit had been busy for many years and we issued invitations to many dancers who joined us-coming from New Hampshire, Massachusetts, Connecticut and New York.

A Powwow requires much planning. The first two or three years, it was a one-day event. Verna suggested that we move the Powwow from York Days and hold it the following weekend. We agreed to this new date but kept the one day time frame. Overnight camping on the field was prohibited and the vehicle traffic was held to an absolute minimum, so our traders had to lug their goods and equipment from the parking area onto the field. This was difficult for them but it enabled us to offer an "old time" Powwow with no vehicles behind the booths to detract from the traditional aspect. For a number of years, we were able to maintain this parking arrangement.

There was no camping on the field and most of the local campgrounds were filled at this time of the summer. We were invited, (again through the kindness and help of Verna Rundlett) to camp at Kuhn Park (owned by Terry Phillips) which is about 2 miles from the field. It was a beautiful camping area. There was a natural amphitheater with a small stage and plenty of parking spaces and fresh water was provided. Many of the participants came in on Friday night, danced on Saturday and spent the evening Saturday and went home on Sunday.

The first year, after both programs had been completed, all were invited back to Kuhn Park for a feast. For the many years that York Beach Powwow entertained the community, we provided the traditional feast on Saturday evening. The first year was probably the most memorable in that the food was prepared and served in the woods, after dark, at Kuhn Park. Harriett was in charge of planning and a number of volunteers including Don Brennan and Herb Johnson helped cook, serve and clean up afterward. We probably went to our campsites or campers close to midnight. A very successful program, but we did find that this feast arrangement was almost impossible so late in the day. It seemed as if every mosquito in the State of Maine found its way to Kuhn Park after 10:00 in the evening.

As the years went by, so many people came on a regular basis that they had developed local friendships, favorite campgrounds and inns, hotels and motels in the area and had settled very comfortably into the fabric of York Beach. Kuhn Park had served us well in the early years but unfortunately we no longer had this accommodation, as it was for sale.

From the very first program, it seemed that the York Beach Powwow was destined to become a tradition. One of our initial tasks was to find and invite as many Maine Natives as possible. Coming from out of state as we were, we did not want to offend the local Natives. It is our feeling that a Powwow is primarily a social event with many traditional overtones and it was necessary to have these people with us. Ed, working with the advertising committee, of course, spent much time traveling and making telephone calls in an effort to include as many area Natives as possible.

One of Ed's first stops was at the Moccasin Shop at Wells, Maine where he invited Chief Tomekin and family to join us. He wanted them to enjoy the festivities and set up a booth to sell their wares if they wished. He also contacted Princess Running Water (Penobscot) who was living in Wells, Maine at the time and she was willing to lend her support. Ruth Johnson (Penobscot) and her family set up with their traditional State of Maine Native crafts, baskets, wood carvings, etc. Stan Neptune came down from Old Town with his museum quality wood carvings and set up a very attractive display. Stan's sister Janice Galipeau set up with her quillwork jewelry. We were delighted to include so many Maine Natives.

Lynne Bessette, who operates Silver Hawk in Ashburnham, Massachusetts, had a large display of crafts featuring Eastern Woodland items. Dick and Terry Naslund came with their Southwestern jewelry and their Hopi carvings. Chief One Bear (Raymond Tremblay) set up his pottery display. Elk Dog (Mike Pratt) set up with his interesting assortment of knives and other handcrafted items.

I had attended the Wampanoag Powwow on the 4th of July in Mashpee, Massachusetts where I met Fire Woman (Jackie Emerton) and she graciously came to our Powwow and set up for many years. She gave us further Maine representation. Ed also set up a stand with his goods from *the little bull*. Always, from beginning to end, Princess Winona attended every Powwow. The Wandering Bull joined these other traders with a booth featuring books and craft supplies.

Our goal had always been to have a nice assortment of traders but not so many that they would be competing with each other with similar products. There were many traders over the years who wished to join us. Unfortunately, we had to put them on the waiting list until someone else was unable to return. It was important that the traditional Powwow atmosphere be maintained.

A Powwow requires that you have a number of traders; music, of course, is most important, as well as dancers in a variety of traditional outfits. We personally invited dancers to join us and encouraged them to wear their outfits when in the circle. We had established a reputation for having good dancers and rewarded these dancers by preserving the integrity of the dance circle. It was our feeling that these people spent many hours during the year making their outfits and they deserved the opportunity to display their talents. In an effort to get dancers to attend, we called Chief White Wolf (Lee Maddix), head of the Dighton Intertribal Indian Council, who willingly gathered a group of dancers from Southeastern Massachusetts. Lee and his family and friends joined us in the dance circle. Lee really came through for us.

The dance circle itself consisted of bales of hay from local Blaisdell Farm, around the perimeter (probably the same ones used on the float in the parade). We found that the hay was an excellent way of outlining our circle and we did this for many years. Ropes and stakes, which are used at many Powwows, give the impression that the public is not welcome nor invited into the circle. In addition, they tend to interfere with picture taking. The hay made it a little less formal and a bit more inviting.

As the years went by, we were unable to obtain the hay and had to resort to the stake and rope procedure. I still have the feeling that there might be a better way of doing this.

Occasionally, at a Powwow, I will suggest not having ropes and stakes and it generally works out well – that is one of those "someday" things that I hope to accomplish. As of 2011 we have seen a trend away from using stakes and rope and it is being well received.

We had groups of dancers come in from the Springfield, Massachusetts area and dancers come down from Penobscot country. There was a strong contingent of Indians and Indian veterans who assisted us from New Hampshire. There were so many of our friends who came from Massachusetts, from Connecticut, and from New York – all of these people coming together gave us a very diverse group. Among those early attendees were Elwood Webster, Sly Fox (John Oakley), Many Horses (Marvin Burnett), Kenny and Debbie Alves, George Stryker (Tuscarora), Tall Oak (Eddie Faria).

As time went on some vendors were unable to continue attending and others took their places. Over the years Millie Noble was an enthusiastic supporter. David Little Tree, who was rapidly becoming a renowned silversmith, began attending our Powwows and sold his unique handcrafted silver jewelry.

For many years, the sound system was handled by Ron Perry, who was always ready at the microphone for a fill-in joke or was ready to display his flute-playing talents. In later years, the sound system was handled by Jeff and Brian who provided the same service to many New England events.

The evening program that we opposed doing in our first year became standard as long as the event continued at the ball field. It seemed to be almost as popular as our daytime program. We found that the audience would keep us there late into the evening while enjoying the music and dancing. The applause was enthusiastic and we were unable to conclude the event until it got too dark and the grass became so slippery that we could no longer safely dance. For our dancers, this became one of the most interesting and heartwarming events that any of us had ever experienced.

One year, after our afternoon program and after the evening feast, the weather, which had threatened all day long, developed into a very steady, hard rain and we passed the word as well as we could that the evening program was cancelled. We were standing in Ed's store talking with some folks, when some of the dancers came in to inquire why we were not dancing. We told them of the cancellation due to the weather. Their reply was, "That is all well and good, except that there is a drum set up beneath the pavilion roof with a few dancers and the audience is there, standing outside the pavilion with umbrellas and raincoats waiting for the program to begin." We hustled down to the pavilion to find that this was true. The singers were ready to sing and the dancers had assembled and the audience was there. With no amplification nor microphone and precious few outfits, we did our best to honor the audience with a makeshift program. We usually danced on the grass and not on the cement floor of the pavilion but under the circumstances we did our best to entertain and educate the assembled group. Cement is not a good dance surface. It is very hard on the feet and legs and it tends to wear out moccasins more quickly. This did not seem to slow the dancers or the singers, nor did it quell the enthusiasm of the audience, who stood in the rain for two hours while we performed. Before the program was over, the other drum came down and set up on the other side of the pavilion and we continued with a full scale dancing program sans outfits. We had determined a number of years before that the York Beach audience was the best group in the world to dance for and that thought was solidified that night in the rain.

Each year, the number of the dancers participating grew. The first year, we considered ourselves very fortunate when we were able to showcase twenty five dancers. I am sure that eleven years later the dancers numbered eighty-five to ninety on a regular basis.

Paul - York Beach Powwow, August 1999

A Powwow requires not only talented dancers but also talented singers. White Horse (Ken Hamilton) displayed his singing ability and was accompanied by a number of local singers that first year. After the first year it became apparent that it was necessary to have two or more drums. Our very first invited and host drum was the Four Winds singers from New Hampshire. The Four Winds is a Southern drum and has been singing together for over twenty years. They brought an extensive repertoire, of authentic songs. They continued in attendance every year at our Powwow.

In the New Bedford, Massachusetts area, Paul Levasseur had been training a group of young men who were singing Northern songs, and we invited them the second year. They had become quite accomplished and our Powwow was one of their first gigs. They called themselves The Iron River Singers. Today, many years later, these young men are still singing and are known as one of the best singing groups on the East Coast. The group has expanded; the young men have grown and married and many of their wives also sing on the drum. A number of their children are participating as dancers in Powwows throughout New England. Over the years, other drums joined our Powwow but the Four Winds Singers and The Iron River Singers had the longest standing.

Some of the men who sang with White Horse got together in later years and formed a pick-up drum. The University of New Hampshire was kind enough to supply them with a room in which to practice. Practice locations can be an issue since the drum is very loud and might be a nuisance in a built-up neighborhood. The University room was perfect for this use. The room happened to be room 101. As a result of this practice room number, the drum became known as the 101 Singers.

Other drums came and we were fortunate in that we also had a waiting list of singers who wished to participate. Ideally, three drums would allow us to present a good program while at the same time giving each drum sufficient singing time. It is not exciting for a singer to attend a Powwow and be so far back in rotation that they seldom have an opportunity to "peak." We found that three drums provided the dancers with plenty of dance time, the singers with enough singing time to adequately exhibit their program, and at the same time gave the singers enough break time between songs.

Some of the other drums who came were the Rice Lake Singers from Alderville, Peterborough, Ontario, Canada who journeyed many miles to sing for us for the last two years of the Powwow. This Ojibwa group was lead by Bruce Smoke. The Good Thunder Drum, with Kevin Keene as lead singer, also attended. From time to time other guest drums would honor us with their music.

The traditional way to thank singers and dancers (and their families) for attending the Powwow is to offer a "feast" for all. A feast in our traditional sense of the word can be anything from a hot dog and chips to a full-fledged feast with meat and potatoes and dessert etc. It was our wish always to present a feast - we believe it also encouraged sociability. We offered these feasts on Saturday evening.

The 1997, Powwow was memorable for a different reason. The Saturday morning was perfect and a large crowd had assembled. My usual job as Master of Ceremonies was going smoothly. The opening for the Powwow was on schedule. A woman came up and introduced herself. She was Barbara Ylonen Bonnano from the Village of Arctic Circle in Finland. She was wearing traditional clothing which consisted of a red hat with 4" trim similar to our assumption sash, a blue over-blouse with red trim, a leather possibles bag, and moccasins decorated with fur. We became instant friends and met at many Powwows in Northern New England. Barbara has crossed over since our meeting but I miss her and her stories, which are very similar to those of our indigenous Inuit people. Her daughter and grandson still dance at Maine and New Hampshire gatherings.

We had enjoyed several dances early that Saturday afternoon. I was at the microphone and Ron Perry was sitting nearby, when suddenly I felt terrible. I had no specific ailment but I knew that something was terribly wrong. I asked Ron Perry to get someone to take over and walked quickly to our sales booth. Harriett started to help me remove my choker, bracelets, necklaces, etc. Ernie Proper willingly assumed the Master of Ceremonies duties to keep things moving along. Our son, Dan raced for a paramedic and returned with Leo Flynn from the York Fire Department, who quickly summoned an ambulance and in due time I was taken to York Hospital.

I had seen enough movies and television dramas to be prepared. When the hospital doctor removed the blanket from my legs and saw my elaborately beaded leggings, and said, "What's this?" I feared he would cut them with his big scissors and shouted, "Those are Indian pants - don't cut them." He laughed and proceeded to work his wonders. A heart attack is an awesome assault to one's body, but if you have to have one, being near York Hospital is the optimal place to be. The York Hospital did a great job for my body and my spirits. The care I received for the seven days of hospitalization was world class. The hospital staff was concerned not only for me but for my family as well. My admission to York Hospital was considered the second most exciting story, after the story of the patient who was delivered to the ER in a front end loader during a snowstorm.

Harriett and our kids and friends got us through the Powwow weekend. The event continued thanks to the cooperation and concern of a huge number of people. Many of the family stayed in York for the week. Those who had to return to their jobs drove back and forth to visit on a regular basis. The hospital staff extended their concern to family members as well as to me. Snacks and meals appeared as if by magic! Information was given every step of the way so that the family was always apprised of my course of treatment. The ICU staff welcomed Ed each evening about 10 pm (after he had closed *the little bull*). It was a very difficult time made as comfortable as possible by the caring hospital staff.

A long recuperation followed and I was lost in the world of daytime television. Everyone was generous with good wishes and concern - phone calls, letters, cards, and fruit baskets. Among others, Slow Turtle (John Peters) called to wish me well. A long talk that day got me back into the routine. Slow Turtle crossed over in 1997. I miss him.

We were fortunate to have had a successful Powwow for eleven years. The quality of the Powwow increased and many of the same spectators came every year. Now, many years later we still meet and talk with people who are so proud that they were able to attend every year.

The Saturday night session in 2001 was crowded. The sky was clear, the stars were out, and it was a near full moon. As a final dance, we invited all the dancers and spectators into the circle for a Two Step. The drum increased in intensity, the dancers' enthusiasm was contagious, and the singers and dancers were reluctant to stop. The Four Winds Singers were at their best, the dancers were caught in the spirit of the moment. It was a truly awesome event. Head singer, Paul Burke, wanted to slow the pace down – to maintain control. The enthusiasm was far too intense. As the music faded into the night sky, the dancers and audience reluctantly drifted off, still under the spell of a truly wonderful spirit.

Sunday afternoon, with the memory of that unforgettable night still fresh in our hearts and minds, a decision was made. Paul Burke, lead singer of the Four Winds Singers, called me to the drum, where Ed and his wife, Michelle were standing with tears in their eyes. The time had come. The afternoon session, the last of the weekend, was almost over. At Ed's request I went to the microphone and announced that this was the last

Paul, Theo, Ed, Chris, and Andy at York
Beach Harvest Fest

York Beach Powwow. The Powwow had gotten as big as it could, it had touched the hearts of many people, and the Bullock family and the singers knew that it had gotten as close to our ideal as possible. With heavy hearts, with the joy of friendships made and continued, with the knowledge that many lives had been touched and the comfort of a job well done, the Four Winds sang a final Honor Song. The family danced around the circle and many hugs, kisses, and tears later, the York Beach Powwow ended.

Paul and grandson Theo Bullock at York Beach Harvest Fest

ALASKA 2001

The seeds of our Alaskan adventure were sown at the York Beach Powwow. Gray Wolf (Andre Forest) attended many of our Powwows and came with his wife, Night Dancer (Esther), and their daughters, Bright Star (Heidi Duran) and Morning Star (Chere' Piermarini). The family lives in the Fitchburg, Massachusetts area and they are of Abenaki and MicMac heritage. Andy and Esther also had a son, Standing Bear (Don Forest), who had been living in Alaska for about 25 years.

Don and his wife Edie formed a committee in Alaska to present a "New England Powwow" and Don had asked his father to recommend a singing group and a Master of Ceremonies for this "dream Powwow" that he wanted to present in the Fairbanks, Alaska area. Andy had managed to secure some tapes of the 101 Singers and also of me as Master of Ceremonies.

Don Standing Bear and his father Gray Wolf

We were unaware of this at the time, so it was with surprise and great pleasure that we received an invitation to the Midnight Sun Intertribal Powwow, which was to be held in Fairbanks, Alaska in July of 2001. I was asked to be the Master of Ceremonies and the 101 Singers were an invited drum.

The committee secured a suitable location, and most importantly, requested permission from the local tribal Elders to proceed with this venture.

Our "on the ground" Alaskan Adventure really started when Harriett and I walked out of the airport at 11:30 pm to see a man standing on the sidewalk, reading his newspaper. During our time there, we enjoyed full daylight and it was not unusual to ride along the boulevards and streets and see people sweeping their sidewalks and trimming their lawns and hedges at 11:30 or 12:00 at night. Most of the homes, and certainly all of the tourist facilities, featured a double curtained affair at the windows so that you could adjust for light changes and enjoy sleeping in a darkened room.

The flowers and plants were especially lush at this time of the year. Even the pansies were half again as large as the flowers we see in New England.

The people were very friendly and it was easy to strike up a conversation in the stores and restaurants. We noticed that many people living in Alaska had originally served in the U.S. Military.

Harriett and I were fortunate to be able to arrive about seven days prior to the 2001 Powwow. There were a number of things which we hoped to accomplish in that time. One of them was to help Don Standing Bear visit the newspapers, radio and television stations to work up enthusiasm for the upcoming event. We also had an opportunity to meet the

Elders who had so graciously granted permission to put on the Powwow.

We enjoyed many of the tourist attractions in the area and saw as much as we could. We were able to take a tour on the boat "Discovery," drive to Chena Hot Springs, and attend dog sled races and contests (even though there was no snow). We visited an abandoned gold mine (we found no gold), and took in numerous vacation spots including the Arctic Circle. Traveling about as we did enabled us to become familiar with the area and the local people. We got to know many of the committee members and were invited into their homes.

The committee was very busy - they were making last minute requests for donations and we spent a great deal of time with Don Standing Bear visiting local establishments. The business community was especially helpful - the newspaper interviewed us several times and the radio station and TV stations also did a considerable amount of publicity for us. It certainly appeared to be a very close knit community.

Since this was the first intertribal Powwow in Alaska, the committee was new to the concept and not totally aware of all that was being asked of them. They made up for their lack of experience with their enthusiasm and eagerness to learn.

One of the positions they neglected to include in their planning was the very difficult task of Arena Director. Christopher Charlebois, who was with the New England group, had been invited to entertain at the event with his Native American flute music. Fortunately, Chris agreed to fill in and to serve as Arena Director. Chris helped us line up the various tribal groups for Grand Entry. With his diplomatic approach and communication skills, he was able to observe the necessary personal/tribal traditions which resulted in a very smooth Grand Entry for all.

We had at least 15 dancers and singers with us from New England. Some of our spouses and children were able to attend and they, of course, paid for their own transportation.

The Walking Hawk Singers was the host drum. (Don Standing Bear was a member of this group.) The 101 Singers, a well known New England group, was an invited drum. This drum included Lead Singer Ed Bullock, Ken Hamilton, Dan Bullock, Dustin Boston, Dave Hunt, Bob Durand, Robert Benedetto, Bruce James, Jimmy Waite, Chris Bullock, Liz Charlebois, and Suzie Husted.

The 101 Drum in Fairbanks, Alaska, 2001. Back row – Liz Charlebois, Robert Benedetto, Dan Bullock, Ken Hamilton, Dave Hunt, Chris Bullock, Jimmy Waite, Susie Husted. Front row – Bob Durand, Ed Bullock, Dustin Boston, Bruce James

Walks the Nation, a group of very talented youngsters from the Two Rivers, Alaska area, was also invited to perform. Another drum came to us from Anchorage, Alaska - it was called The Sleeping Lady Drum. Our curiosity got the best of us and we found out that a mountain range near Anchorage had the form of a sleeping lady, hence its name. There were other specialty groups - some Potlatch Dancers, several Eskimo singers and dancers, and other groups of tribal people from the entire state. We met some Aleuts and admired them for having traveled so far to be with us. There also were some people who had flown in from Barrow.

It was our intent to bring Native Americans from the lower 48 and to include all of the First Nation Peoples of Canada, as well as including all of the Alaskan Native tribal groups. It was to be a social event as well as a spiritual happening.

Preceding the Powwow date we had had a week of beautiful summer weather (very much like Massachusetts). The day of the Powwow arrived and the clouds opened up and the rains came along with the wind. Unfortunately, this weather lasted all day and into the evening. The entire Powwow was moved inside to a large exhibition hall. There was room for a large dance circle and all of the vendors, somewhat crowded perhaps, but room enough.

It is interesting to note that on several occasions during our three trips to the Fairbanks area, residents told us that they were not surprised with the rain which drove us indoors since early July was the start of the annual rainy season.

A large supply of folding chairs was available and the committee set up two large circles. The inner circle was for the Elders. Immediately behind that was a circle of chairs for the invited guests. We were very much impressed with the respect shown to the Elders, whether they were Native people or guests. We saw countless examples of this throughout our entire stay in Alaska. Traditionally, the Elders are very much respected and shown the utmost courtesy in every instance. This is true not only in Alaska but throughout the Native community in general.

The Grand Entry was scheduled for noon and we were not sure where all of the dancers came from, but were amazed when they came through the door. Many people came from all over Alaska dressed in their traditional clothing. People from the lower 48 such as we would see at a New England Powwow, Jingle Dancers, Grass Dancers, and Traditional Dancers all joined in the Grand Entry. There were Aleuts, Athabascan, G'wichin, Haida, Tlingit, Eskimos (Inupiat, Yupik) all in their traditional clothing - this was magical.

The Eskimo people were dressed in parkas made of caribou skin and trimmed with fur. They wore the traditional white gloves. Tlingit people were elaborately dressed in their woolen button blankets which were navy blue or black with red borders, contrasted with white pearl buttons applied to the dark wool. They wore straw hats or elaborately carved masks. The Athabascans wore beautiful deerskin clothing adorned with floral beadwork.

The Arena Director organizes the Grand Entry usually with the flags (colors) coming first, followed by the Elder Chiefs, then the men, the women, Jingle Dancers, Fancy Shawl Dancers, and the children. This is not a hard and fast rule and we vary it depending upon the people available for Grand Entry and always look to the committee for guidance in this respect.

Button Blanket – Note the distinctive headpiece

More Button Blankets

The Arena Director has many responsibilities throughout the Powwow. Basically, he or she is a very polite arbitrator and it is the responsibility of the Arena Director to maintain order and decorum, to relay information from the Master of Ceremonies to the drums and dancers, and to act on any necessary function which will enhance the Powwow. He or she must be available at all times to maintain the flow of the Powwow. In Chris' case, the job became more complex because he was not familiar with the Alaskan Powwows. He was not aware that each Alaskan group had a certain place in the entry. A complication arose when certain groups requested that they be first in line in the entry and other groups requested that they be the last to enter. We believe that the Tlingit, upon entry, danced in backwards to display their lovely button blankets and we also think that their method of dancing into the circle was to identify them in terms of clan or position. Chris was so busy as Arena Director that he only had a few opportunities to entertain with his flute.

Many years ago when I was a youngster, an Elder from New York told me that the word "tuxedo" was an Indian word that meant "fancy dress." I have told that story many times and explained to various groups that I was wearing my "tuxedo." That story came to mind as I saw these people from all of these different tribal groups - I felt they were truly wearing their "tuxedos."

The Grand Entry was finally in place and the 101 Singers, who sang the Grand Entry Song, probably went through three songs to accommodate the incoming dancers. The colors (the flags) and the military honor guard leading the Grand Entry were most impressive. The flag bearers were followed by four women who had been selected to further honor the flags in a very Native way. As the honor guard and flag bearers made their way to center circle, all attention was on the flags. The bearers dipped the flags so that the four women could attach the fluffs to the tip of the flag staffs. They remained in the center of the dance circle with the Stars and Stripes upright throughout the Flag Song and the Veteran's Song so that all could honor and respect the flag of our country. The other flags were then brought upright and with military orders the flags were placed in the stanchions which remained in the center of the dance circle until the conclusion of the program. The color bearers, honor guard, and the four women completed the circle by dancing to the entrance. This was all accomplished with military precision and was a most moving honoring. Harriett had been selected as one of the four women and was very pleased and honored to have been chosen. Don Standing Bear's sisters were also so honored. Ed remembers an impressive round of applause following the flag song – this was something new to us and we were impressed with the crowd's display of patriotism.

The first intertribal was sung by the 101 singers and this first song was most successful in bringing out all people to fill the dance arbor. It was a pleasure watching all these folks dance in their own style. The Powwow had begun.

We had a long table set up with microphones for the Master of Ceremonies, the Arena Director and a young lady named Graehl. Graehl's job was to help me pronounce some of the names which were very unfamiliar to me. She was also adept at giving me tribal information so that I would know a little bit about the history of the various tribes and peoples. We attempted to maintain access to this table at all times.

As a rule, I stand when I am the Master of Ceremonies and

Paul and Graehl Brooks, his right hand gal

I was certainly standing at this Grand Entry. When I went back to my seat at the table, I was quite surprised to find that my chair was occupied. There was an elderly Eskimo lady sitting in my place. I explained to her that in order to act as the Master of Ceremonies, I needed to be able to get to my chair so that I could use the microphone and have access to my notes. I offered to get her another chair where she could watch the dancing and be comfortable. She shook her head and said, "This is my chair." I tried again, a little bit more diplomatically, to explain to her how important it was that I could get to my papers on the table. Additionally, I needed to be able to confer with Graehl so that I would know who the dancers were and so I could carry out my duties as Master of Ceremonies. I offered her another chair. This elderly Eskimo woman only shook her head and said, "This is my chair." Certainly it was not my intent to forcibly remove her and I did enjoy talking with her and at no point was she interested in giving up "her chair." She held forth until the Powwow was almost over and then she disappeared into the crowd.

Every group present was allowed an opportunity to dance or sing in their own style or tradition. The Tlingits in their button blankets were most enthusiastic and danced frequently. Athabascan groups put on their exhibition using a long piece of calico held by the dancers. We had a number of children's groups doing their own special numbers.

The Eskimo people came into the circle. They had a single-headed drum, which was approximately 19" in diameter and about an inch and a half deep with a handle that made the drum look something like a large fry pan. The Eskimos not only sang but they danced and drummed at the same time. They danced by raising one leg, placing it back on the floor, then the other leg was raised so that it was almost a hopping motion. The singing was done with a great deal of enthusiasm and the drumstick hit the head of the drum. On occasion, the drumstick was brought up from underneath and hits the frame only - not hitting the head at all. The Eskimo people truly enjoyed being in the center circle, singing and dancing. Even though the beat was quite a bit different for the other dancers, all of the dancers managed to get into the circle and dance. The beat was different, the music was different, but the enthusiasm was overwhelming.

Graehl asked me if I would meet some Eskimo women who had asked if they could sing. She brought me over to three elderly Eskimo women who did not speak much English. She introduced me to each of them in turn and we shook hands and hugged. Graehl said that they would like to sing for the whole group; furthermore, they would like to sing three songs. I explained to Graehl and the women that we had so many things in our program that we unfortunately did not have time for three songs but we could accommodate one song if they would like to do that. They all shook their heads and said, "No! Three songs!" This went on for 10 minutes or so and I finally gave up and invited them to sing whatever they would like. They walked out into the center of the circle and started singing. Their voices were high pitched. As soon as they began, everybody raced to the center of the circle and started dancing. At that particular point, all semblance of organization was lost. Everyone was dancing, these three women were singing as loud as they could, and the music went on and on. It was the most thrilling thing that the New Englanders had ever seen. They indeed sang their three songs and again everyone, young people, old people, middle aged people were all out in the circle – it didn't matter whether they were Eskimo or Aleut or from the lower 48. It did not matter where they were from, everybody was dancing and everybody was singing. It was one of the most exciting moments of the Powwow.

The Athabascan dancers

Ken Hamilton leading the 101 Singers in a Stomp Dance

The Stomp Dances that the New England group brought to Alaska were very popular and people did not hesitate at all to get to the end of the dance line to participate. A lead song was usually sung by White Horse (Ken Hamilton) and the repeat was promptly given by all of the dancers who followed. Whenever we had an opportunity, we called for a Stomp Dance which would immediately pick up the tempo of the Powwow. It was obvious that the Alaskan dancers enjoyed their music loud and fast.

With the help of the Arena Director we arranged to have individual groups and organizations participate in a schedule that assured we would have a variety of offerings. This was somewhat difficult since we were not always sure just what each group wished to do. Graehl was a big help in this regard.

Taking pictures outdoors was very difficult due to the rainy weather and the lighting inside did not lend itself to photography. We had hoped to take many photographs of these very wonderful people and their beautiful outfits, but were not able to get as many pictures as we had wanted.

We were invited to a feast which was to be held at the conclusion of the afternoon program, in a small kitchen and picnic area. As the Powwow ended and the public was leaving, Harriett and I got involved in many conversations with people about the Powwow. We completely lost track of time and had totally forgotten about the feast. A committee member came looking for us and said, "Hey, you people are supposed to be down at the feast." We had no idea where we should be and our guide graciously agreed to escort us to the area of the feast. When we arrived, we were aware that everyone who had been invited was in place and waiting for us. We were quite embarrassed that we had not been prompt and had kept everyone waiting. We were taken to the head of the line with an escort from the committee, who served us. We were told it would be their pleasure to do so. As we walked through the line, our escorts filled our plates according to our choice. We were amazed at the variety of foods offered at this feast, prepared by volunteers. In addition to fish prepared in so many different ways, there were all types of traditional foods. After going through the line, we were seated at a picnic table which had been reserved for us and members of the committee circulated around us to be certain that we did not want for anything. The feast was spectacular and we were amazed at the amount of work that the committee went through to prepare such an excellent meal.

Our celebration after the Powwow, 2001. Clockwise from the front - Paul, Liz and Chris Charlebois, Susie Husted, Ken Hamilton, Carl Bullock, Dan, Ed and Michelle Bullock, Jimmy Waite, Dustin Boston, Bruce James, Bob Durant, Dave Hunt, Chris Bullock, Laura and Robert Benedetto, Harriett Bullock

Feast after the Powwow, 2001 – Andy Forest, Chere' Piermarini, Harriett, Paul, Esther Forest

We were very fortunate to be able to attend the Midnight Sun Intertribal Powwow in 2001, 2002, and 2004. The Powwow was not held in 2003. When looking back at these Powwows, it seemed to us that the 2001 Powwow was the most successful, although we had a number of weather situations which caused us to deviate from the planned program. It was my honor to act as Master of Ceremonies at all three Powwows.

The singers from Kenai Peninsula. Sophie, Angie, and Marion join three of the Navajo Code Talkers, 2004

In 2004, the city of Fairbanks invited a group of Navajo Code Talkers to the city to help celebrate Independence Day. These gentlemen and their families were invited to spend time with us at the Powwow and we enjoyed meeting with them and their families. Some of them had wives, children and/or grandchildren with them and we were able to spend a considerable amount of time together. They did not dance with us but their families did join in and the Code Talkers were able to enjoy listening to the music and watching the dancers.

Of course, in July of 2001 we had no idea that in a few weeks the country would be shattered with the news of 9/11 – airplanes crashing into buildings and thousands of Americans dying – that the world would be changed forever.

CHIEF MARIE SMITH JONES

One of the special things about travel is the friends made and the memories shared. A very important friendship began on the first day of our very first Midnight Sun Intertribal Powwow in Alaska. This is the story as told to us by our son Eyes That Shine (Ed), who brought the 101 Singers to perform at that first Powwow.

As Ed tells us, he was positioned in the lead singer's spot at the 101 drum, preparing to sing the opening song of this very momentous Powwow. When looking around the large room filled with many Alaskan Natives of various tribes and affiliations, his eyes fell upon an elderly lady who was looking right back at him.

The Powwow was in full swing, singers singing, dancers dancing, and still this woman continued to gaze at him. The first opportunity he had, he was in the dance circle enjoying the music and the dance. His concentration was interrupted by a young lady dancing beside him - she had been seated next to the mystery woman. A brief conversation identified this older woman as Chief Marie, chief of the Eyak nation and the only person fluent in the Eyak language. Ed was quite amazed that Chief Marie (at the tender age of roughly 85 or 86) would have traveled all the way from Anchorage to attend this event and furthermore, that she wanted to speak with him. As soon as his duties as lead singer permitted, he went to introduce himself to her. As he said, "It was an instant love affair." They had this instant attraction and he spent as much time as possible with her and her companion, Shelah. Each time he could join her, he brought her a present as was befitting an Elder - a bottle of water, a bit of food.

The 101 singers gather around Chief Marie, 2001

Every time they talked, she shared stories from her life. He was learning about her and her tribe. The following day (Sunday) Chief Marie asked Ed to invite the drum and the group with whom he was traveling to her campsite for a feast.

The feast of smoked salmon and Fritos was shared by all (this was reminiscent of the story of the loaves and fishes from Biblical Times). The food was shared, but more importantly, the stories were shared. The life story of the amazing woman was unfolding. She sat at her campsite smoking one cigarette after another, stuffing the discards into an old fashioned Coke bottle. She did not want to be cautioned about smoking - what harm was it going to do her now? I was concerned that she might inadvertently forget and try to drink from the same bottle. Her entire attitude was very realistic - she did not pull any punches.

This gathering was very interesting - we all sat around listening to Chief Marie, captivated by this marvelous new friend who had a story to share and share it she did. Although she lived in Anchorage at that time, her home was Cordova, Alaska.

Chief Marie was a minimalist. Shelah told how they would travel to gatherings or Powwows, planning to be gone for a week or two. Chief Marie would set out with a small handbag of necessities and berate Shelah for all of the equipment she felt was essential. This was totally unlike Princess Winona, who must have brought everything she owned to Powwow!

Chief Marie told us that during World War II, the United States government brought Alaskan natives into internment camps for "their own safety." These camps were far from the Natives' home and in her case, she and her husband were taken to separate camps and their children to a third camp. These

Chief Marie and Paul in conversation after the Powwow – Note her everpresent cigarette

camps had none of the essentials – even the shelters were leaking. The Natives were cold and hungry and many times ill. When the war ended, the Natives were released without any attempt to help them assimilate back into society. This, she said, was her downfall. She became the stereotypical drunken Indian, living on the streets, begging for money, sleeping under bridges. At some point, in a moment of clarity, she realized that this life was not helping her or her tribe. She "cleaned herself up" and became a driving force for Native issues. Within a very short time she was flown to New York City to speak at the United Nations on Native Rights. She spoke to this group on two different occasions. She did not mince words.

Shelah had long been a companion to Chief Marie. She assisted her in a myriad of ways. Driving her to gatherings was one of her responsibilities. She helped with the shopping and most anything that needed doing. This enabled Shelah, Chief Marie's adopted daughter, to have access to many places which would have been denied her under other circumstances. They had an informal personal relationship – more "I'm just helping this lady out – Yah, she is the Chief – but I am just helping her out."

Ed left Fairbanks after the Powwow with promises to keep in touch and he did in fact keep in touch with Chief Marie and Shelah.

Ed told us about calling Chief Marie one day and during the conversation he asked when her birthday was so he could send her a card. She informed him that it was that very day and he congratulated himself for calling on such a special day, only to have her laugh and say, "Yah every day is my birthday." She said, "Send me a card everyday because every day is my birthday. "

In 2002, the Midnight Sun Powwow was held inside again due to the weather. Chief Marie, Shelah, and one other lady approached Ed early on to tell him that they had to talk to him. They went out to a wooded area adjacent to the parking lot. Chief Marie reminded Ed who she was and her role as Chief. They talked about the Eyak nation and its song, telling Ed that as Chief, she was responsible for keeping the Eyak people and their culture alive and strong. No one outside Alaska had ever been given the song and it was time that the song be given away. "I am giving you this song," she said, "if you will accept this song, I will ask that you tell my story and sing this song to anyone who will listen."

So there they were, out in the woods, singing the Eyak national anthem over and over so that Ed could learn it. One of the security people came to investigate the noise and was told by Chief Marie to ignore them and let them continue. Smart man that he was, he followed her advice. Since that day, Ed has told her story a hundred times and sung her song as she asked. She trusted Ed with the song and her story and it has been his honor and privilege to share it with others.

Chief Marie and the 101 singers gather at her feast, 2001

Ed Bullock, Chief Marie, and Shelah

Giving a song in the Native culture is a very significant thing. It is both an honor and a responsibility to have a song gifted to you. It is generally understood that Native American music is governed under "Native Copyright." A song can be given away by a member of a tribe with the authority to do so. The rules are clear to anyone who is honorable and unclear to anyone looking to abuse them for their own purposes, according to Ed.

Ed, Chief Marie, and Chris in 2005 for her birthday party

Ed continued to be in contact with both Chief Marie and Shelah. In 2005 the tribe and the village of Chickaloon planned a celebration to present Chief Marie with a moose hide dress (she had never had one). They made her a white moose hide dress beaded in the floral Athabascan style. When asked what she wanted for this party, Chief Marie responded that she wanted Ed and the 101 Singers to join the celebration. It was not possible to have the entire drum attend but Ed and his brother One Feather (Chris) flew to Anchorage for the event, which was held in the Alaskan Native Heritage Center. The building was jammed with 800-1000 people in every nook and cranny of this large building. Many dignitaries spoke and many, many chiefs honored this amazing woman- it was a BIG THING. When it was time for the Eyak National Anthem, this fellow from Maine who had been flown in began to sing and Diane Little Eagle (a friend of Chief Marie's) joined him. Soon, hundreds were singing to honor Chief Marie and her tiny nation. Ed had been taught to sing this with a big smile, good thoughts, and in a positive manner. That is what he did and it was right no matter how it was done, because it was done for her. As soon as the song was complete Chief Marie presented Ed with a Dentalium Shell Necklace, which in her culture is a significant gift. It means "you are family. " It was a magical moment - a never-to-be-forgotten time for a very special woman.

A huge give-away followed the ceremony which is a clear indication of the esteem in which Chief Marie was held. A give-away can take a variety of forms due to different customs. It may involve expensive and extravagant gifts or small tokens of appreciation, but basically it is an effort to indicate how revered and respected the honored individual is. The value of the gifts is usually less important than the honor which is being shown.

On January 21, 2008, we lost our dear friend when Chief Marie crossed over at 89 years of age. Per her request she was buried in her white moose hide wedding dress. She said that she wanted to be dressed appropriately and ready to marry God when she got to Heaven.

It is relationships such as this that made these trips very special and unique for our family. These experiences cannot be duplicated.

BARROW, ALASKA

On our third trip to Alaska, in July 2004, Harriett and I decided to take a side trip to Barrow. We were attracted by the publicity that we saw extolling the virtues of spending a day in Barrow. We made reservations and were pleased when we discovered that the community of Barrow was celebrating a week-long Independence Day program consisting of various activities, fashion shows, dancing exhibitions, and contests. We boarded a Boeing 737 commercial jet aircraft for the flight from Fairbanks to Barrow.

Barrow is the northern-most community in the United States and we were cautioned to dress very warmly. There are no land routes to Barrow – access is only via air or sea. The aircraft was divided so that the forward portion was partitioned off with a chicken wire arrangement for supplies and the passengers were seated in the rear half of the plane. The airline was the lifeline for the people of Barrow. These daily flights carried every type of equipment or food that the Barrow community needed or wanted. We were amazed to see the types of things being transported. There were earth-moving devices, numerous cases of canned foods, perishable items such as milk, and personal items - snow shovels, snow blowers, refrigerators, stoves, and small cages housing a number of sled dogs.

The flight lasted approximately an hour and a half and as we deplaned, it was a brisk 27 degrees and it was snowing. The ground was covered with that white stuff.

A school bus was waiting for us and the driver was quite

personable and eager to show us Barrow. The young man had attended college at the University of Alaska in Fairbanks. When fishing season arrived, he could no longer remain in the "city." He had to fish. Conducting tours became his livelihood while fishing was his passion. We were able to enjoy our guided tour and the young man was quite entertaining and informative. When we reached an intersection of two streets with a traffic light, he told us that the light never changed but it was felt that Barrow should have at least one traffic signal.

The welcome sign in Barrow, Alaska, July, 2004. It was snowing

We passed huge puddles of water that would not soak into the earth due to the permafrost. We saw homes where seals were displayed on the porches or on platforms in the front yard, ready to be butchered. When we returned from our tour, we saw elderly people standing in line with heavy-duty black trash bags. The young people would share a substantial portion of seal meat with the Elders of the community. It was obvious that the Elders came first and as the meat was apportioned, they carried their bag over their shoulders to their homes. In cases where the Elders were not able to carry this much weight, a young man or woman was ready to help them.

We visited the "End of the Road," where Barrow meets the Arctic Ocean. It impressed me that the shore was level with the ocean - there were no rocks, just sand and a large body of water, with huge pieces of ice that had broken loose and drifted freely in the cold ocean.

Many of the people had sled dogs, sometimes only three or four, but sometimes there were 29 or 30, each with their own personal dog house. The dogs were obviously very happy, well fed, and very active. Since we were there in the summertime, we were not able to see dog teams race. In Fairbanks, we saw a dog team race over the soft, slippery grass. Because of the ground cover in Barrow we were not able to see the sleds in action - it was apparent however, these dogs loved to run and they loved to pull the sled. This seemed to be their claim to fame.

The Fourth of July celebrations were held at a local school. Competitions were held in a very large gymnasium. They had huge rolls of plastic unrolled on the floor. At every five or six feet, a woman was seated on the plastic and was given a large fish. These fish were probably 15 - 20 inches long. The women would not only clean and de-scale the fish but they would do it very rapidly with a circular knife called an "ulu." The "ulu" is an Inupiat Eskimo knife - a half circle, which is very sharp. The competition was keen and the audience was cheering the competitors exuberantly - especially when their favorite was ready to present her fish to the judge. The gym was crowded with people and it was not unusual to see babies sound asleep in a type of long sack in which the mother carried her baby on her back. The excitement did not wake the children however, and those who were asleep remained asleep.

The plastic was placed on the floor again and another 25 or 30 women were given a duck, complete with feathers. They were responsible for totally removing each feather from the duck and again preparing the duck for cooking. There were numerous other contests as well and the audience celebrated Independence Day with a great deal of enthusiasm.

The school gym was very large for an elementary school, partly because the community used it for a gathering place but essentially because most of the physical education was done indoors. There was a small outdoor playground surrounded by a very high and very sturdy fence to keep out the polar bears. The danger from polar bears in this extreme northern climate made indoor physical education necessary.

We were able to visit a number of commercial establishments and found that the bread, milk, candy, etc. were extremely expensive. We also had an opportunity to visit "PePe's North of the Border" which was a full-service restaurant featuring Mexican food. We were glad to have a chance to sit where it was warm and enjoy a meal, although it did seem strange to us to be doing it in a Mexican atmosphere.

I was brought up in Bristol, Rhode Island and I seldom missed an opportunity to enjoy all of the things which a Bristol Fourth of July presents to the world. It was a wonderful opportunity to share this Fourth of July with the residents of Barrow. We found that the enthusiasm and the friendliness of the Eskimo people were contagious and we spent a considerable amount of time talking to local residents, who were most interested in explaining their lifestyle to us.

After a most enjoyable and enlightening day, we boarded our plane and in a short while we were back in Fairbanks. I came away with the feeling that all of these people were glad to be able to show us their lifestyle and we look back on our visit as an opportunity to celebrate a part of America which we had not seen before.

We returned to our motel and made plans for our Fourth of July celebration with the Navajo Code Talkers and an opportunity to again put on an intertribal Powwow in the State of Alaska.

AREA GROUPS

THE ORDER FOR THE PRESERVATION OF INDIAN CULTURE (TOPIC)

TOPIC was founded in 1976 by Chief One Bear (Raymond Tremblay) and his wife Little Fawn (Margaret). It was Chief One Bear's feeling that the Native people in the Boston, Massachusetts area should be able to celebrate Native American traditions. The group would be open to all who were interested regardless of their heritage. It was their plan to teach Native American culture. Early on we joined this group.

The first TOPIC Powwow was held in 1976 at Pond Meadow Park (Weymouth/Braintree, Massachusetts). Subsequent Powwows were held at The Paddocks in Canton,

Massachusetts and for a number of years this group celebrated their Powwow at the South Shore Natural Science Center in Norwell, Massachusetts. In recent years the Meditech organization has provided the use of their beautiful grounds for Powwows. The setting near Blue Hills in Canton, Massachusetts is most fitting for this event.

The TOPIC organization has sponsored a scholarship program available to all members upon their high school graduation and has presented each graduate with a check to be used to help defray the cost of future endeavors. The organization has been active in supporting cultural, civic, and patriotic causes.

The Two Step at Topic Powwow in 1994

Chief One Bear served in the United States Army (Artillery) during World War II and the noise from the heavy weapons contributed to One Bear's hearing deficit. He was able to continue to run the organization for 37 years even though his hearing worsened over time, making communication difficult.

Predeceased by his wife Little Fawn, Chief One Bear died on March 6, 2013. The TOPIC organization (his dream) was fully realized and he was active within the organization until a few months before his passing. The organization is a strong and viable one and Chief One Bear's grandson Craig Tremblay is now the Chief. Craig's first Powwow was in 2013 and we are sure that the future looks bright for the group.

WOLLOMONUPPOAG INDIAN COUNCIL

Chief Big Thunder (Frederick Reynolds) of Plainville, Massachusetts was very active in the American Indian Federation and had been a member of that organization for many years. He was interested in forming an organization which would be active in Southeastern Massachusetts. A group of people came together and set up an organization to be called The Wollomonuppoag Indian Council. Accordingly, the charter is dated August 27, 1974 and lists the names of the Charter Members. It includes my name.

The American Legion in Plainville, Massachusetts generously donated the use of their hall for meetings. In 1975, Fred asked the American Legion for permission to use the very small area behind their hall for the group's first Powwow. The Legion obliged and we planned advertising and proceeded to prepare the grounds for our first Powwow. This area of the grounds had not been maintained for some time and we also found that there was a gradual hill behind the Legion Post - dancing up hill is tough. The grass was about 12 inches high and we spent a considerable amount of time preparing the area. Things certainly were a lot simpler in those days, particularly in terms of permits and local governmental requirements. Our publicity worked and we asked Star and Clear Sky and their family to help us out with music. We had a most successful first Powwow.

The Welcome Dance at the Wollomonuppoag Powwow, Wrentham, MA, 1984

The subsequent years found our fledgling organization at a number of different locations and for many years the Powwow has been held at the La Salette Shrine Fairgrounds on route 118 in Attleboro, Massachusetts. The 39th Powwow was held in 2013.

Following Chief Big Thunder's passing Chief Running Deer (John Brin) assumed leadership. Under his guidance the Medicine Society was formed. The group continues to flourish under the current Chief Hawk Eye (Mark Brintnall).

GLICA

GREATER LOWELL INDIAN CULTURAL ASSOCIATION

Onkwe Tase (Ed Guillemette) was born and raised in Dracut, Massachusetts. As a young man he fought in World War II in the European Theater from May 1943 to January 1946. This included D-Day. His service to his country completed, he became active in the Native culture.

In 1961, Ed formed GLICA, an intertribal group comprised of people of many nations who were living in the Lowell/Dracut area. It was my privilege to be part of this group even though I lived somewhat out of the geographical area.

Ed felt that land acquisition was an important aspect of the Native culture and worked very diligently in this regard. In 1978, after a six year battle, the group obtained 150 acres of land, which was to be used for ceremonies and gatherings, then began the task of clearing an area for this purpose. The old adage "many hands make light work" came into play at

Onkwe Tase

this time. I am not sure that the work was ever made light but certainly many hands worked. This land in the Lowell, Dracut, Tyngsboro State Forest became a focal point for the group's activities. Powwows, programs and events were held on a regular basis, both in the forest and at area venues.

Later, the group formed a relationship with the Bedford Veteran's Administration Hospital and for many years, two Powwows have been held at this location annually. Originally, the Powwow at the VA Hospital was held in conjunction with a Native Conference which was being held there as well.

Throughout this time, Ed has spent many hours teaching Iroquois Social Dances such as the Snake Dance and the Friendship Dance. Stomp Dances have been a highlight of the group's events.

The organization is now being led by Chief Eagle Rising (Tom Libby). In its mission statement GLICA states in part: "Our strength lies in our diversity and our ability to live in the present while holding on to the past and looking forward to the future of our people."

New England has been fortunate in recent years to have a number of groups that foster and promote Native American culture. Chief White Wolf (Lee Maddix) was instrumental in founding the Dighton Intertribal Indian Council in Dighton, Massachusetts. This group has been working to preserve the Council Oak tree located nearby. They have a very suitable hall which provides them a meeting place and a location to display some of their memorabilia. They sponsor a number of Powwows throughout the year, as well as socials and fundraisers.

The Worcester area has The Worcester Inter-tribal Indian Center, founded in 1981. This group meets on a regular basis and sponsors an annual Powwow which is open to the public. Led by Chief Gentle Hawk (John Joubert) this is an active, vibrant group whose members frequently attend other Powwows, sharing their talents in terms of music and dancing.

The New Hampshire Inter-tribal Native American Council is located in the Laconia, New Hampshire area. They sponsor a number of Powwows throughout the year both in New Hampshire and Maine. There is a strong social service component to this group and an emphasis on Veterans.

The Massachusetts Center for Native American Awareness was founded by Burne Stanley Peters and her late husband Slow Turtle (John Peters) in 1989. This group sponsors several Powwows and other events throughout the year. They are a driving force within the Native community, sponsoring scholarships, providing heating assistance, and assistance with basic needs. Their leadership group is active and hard working, whether the task is fundraising, community outreach, or cleaning up after a dinner or social. I have been a member of this organization for many years and assist them whenever I am able.

Not really under the heading of "Groups" but important to mention, are the Native tribes in the area which have been active in sponsoring Powwows for many, many years. The Wampanoag Tribe, the Narragansett Tribe, and the Nipmuck Tribe have all hosted Powwows for many years and continue to sponsor events every summer. These are open to the public and provide the community in general an opportunity to experience a Native Powwow.

MT. KEARSARGE INDIAN MUSEUM (MKIM)

Written by Andy Bullock

Powwows have introduced us to all kinds of people. Each new friend opened a whole world of exploration. Such was our first contact with "the guy in the straw hat." We often attended Powwows on the North Shore and New Hampshire in the mid-1970's. It was at such a Powwow that we spied "the guy in the straw hat," walking across the field. On either side of him were elderly women in flowing skirts and lace bonnets. Never in a hurry, they visited each booth, studied the Powwow arbor, and chatted with everyone. Our chance meetings became more frequent, and animated.

"The guy in the straw hat" was Charles (Bud) Thompson. His companions were Shaker Sisters from the Canterbury Shaker Village in New Hampshire. In his quest to learn about music of utopian communities, Bud embraced the community of Canterbury Shaker Village. Bud and his wife Nancy lived with the Shakers and ultimately helped the Sisters develop the Village into a sustainable non-profit organization.

Bud Thompson with his "hat" and
ever-present smile.

Bud has always had a deep respect and understanding of Native America. As an early environmentalist, Bud was concerned about the destruction of the planet. War, pollution, poverty, and injustice were destroying the very core of our country. Bud realized that Native philosophy addressed many of these concerns. He recited Native orators who preached the importance of honoring Mother Earth. These were values he shared...and lived by. In addition to his philosophic views, Bud has a keen knowledge of plants and how they are used for food, medicine and ceremony. As a boy, Bud explored the natural world. He learned how to identify and harvest the bounty of the forest. Bud was interested in how these plants could be used to restore the natural balance of the environment.

Bud describes his early meeting with Chief Sachem Silver Star as a life-altering experience. From that meeting on, Bud began an exploration into Native spirituality, culture, and philosophy. He read voraciously and delved into the deeper context of social and environmental concerns faced by Native Americans. Collecting Native antiques and art was a natural outgrowth of his passion. Soon, his collection outgrew his home in Shaker Village. Baskets, moccasins, pottery, quillwork, books, carvings, and beaded clothing began to appear every time Bud returned from an outing. The word was out. Bud had begun to amass an impressive collection of Native Art. The Shaker Sisters came to the rescue, offering the second floor of the old Shaker Schoolhouse as an area to display this treasure trove.

From those early meetings with Bud, it was clear that he had ideas...big ideas. Every conversation revolved around his vision, a "Museum With a Voice." He was not interested in amassing "a mausoleum of pickled artifacts." Every article he acquired had a place in telling the story delivered by Chief Sachem Silver Star. Bud would visit our booth at Powwows, looking for unique items: a buffalo hide for the Plains exhibit, a porcupine quill loom for the Woodlands display.

Quick with a joke or two, Bud soon became part of our family circle. He was never at a loss for words - many an afternoon was spent chatting and laughing over coffee at the local diner. As the museum began to develop, we met often to discuss his ideas and philosophy. We occasionally made humble suggestions and did our best to share Bud's mission with our Native Community. Many of those early meetings secured lasting bonds between the museum and local Native groups.

Nancy and Bud Thompson

On one late spring visit, Bud revealed that he had secured a location...a home...for his family and the museum. On early visits to the Warner, New Hampshire site, it was clear that Bud had "more vision" than we had. Walking through the "Museum," we saw that the wind easily blew up the dust from the barn floor. It wasn't dark inside since the sun shone through the walls, and roof in many places.

Yes, he had "vision." As the Museum took shape, we continued to visit, suggest, share, introduce, and laugh with Bud. As the building was being renovated, Bud began to think about the interior of the museum. He knew what he wanted to display, but realized he needed fixtures. Coincidentally, we were in the final stages of purchasing Plume Trading & Sales Co. As part of that purchase, we had obtained all of the displays, cases, and office equipment they housed. We had a warehouse full...yes, enough to outfit the museum...and then some. Bud came to Attleboro to look at the cases. Yes, he thought they would work well. After some horse trading, lunch and a lot of laughs, the cases were headed to New Hampshire. Bud rented a truck to transfer the cases. He wondered how they would ever be transported. On a cold, snowy day, Ed and I loaded the truck. Dad and Bud fussed, suggested, cautioned and laughed...and laughed. The truck barely made it up the hill in Warner, finally turning into the muddy path leading to the storage barn. When the last case was slid into place, the doors barely closed.

Bud continues to tell the story of those cases and how they became available at the perfect moment for the Museum. Many of the furnishings, display cases and artifacts at Mt. Kearsarge Indian Museum came from The Wandering Bull. Bud is not shy about sharing these stories about the founding of the Museum.

To this day, Bud walks through the Museum pointing out the influences that the Bullocks had in making his dream become reality. We were honored to help develop and organize the first Powwows at the Museum...suggesting participants, drums, MC's, vendors, and physical arrangements. The Mt. Kearsarge Indian Museum's Powwow has blossomed into one of the premiere dances in New England.

The Bullocks have shared Bud's dream and passion for the Mt. Kearsarge Indian Museum, serving in various roles:

Members, Trustees, Powwow committee, Collections Committee, Deputy Director, display designers, gift shop vendors, restoration specialists and donors. Bud has summed up our relationship in this way..."I never met a Bullock I didn't like."

OUR CHILDREN

At the outset of this project, I felt very strongly that our six adult children who had traveled this road with us, should have the opportunity to participate in the creation of this book in whatever way they were able.

Our eldest, Betsey, while always being supportive in every way, early on had less chance to become deeply involved in the Native Culture. Her age and interests with school, work, and friends saw her on the periphery of this great adventure of ours. Although willing to help with the sewing, finger weaving, and other regalia construction, it was necessary for her to concentrate on other things. Her college years both in Salt Lake City, Utah and Chicago, Illinois, kept her from direct active participation in events at home. In recent years she has been a great help with this manuscript in terms of typing, editing, and keeping me on task.

Those of you who know our son, Gray Hawk (Andy), know him as a man of few words but with a great sense of humor. It was a surprise that he offered many words when asked about his Powwow experiences and the people he met along the way.

His interest in the culture started early on and continues to this day. His education at Trent University in Peterborough, Ontario (Anthropology and Native Studies) and his long term

Our family – Ed, Betsey, Andy, Faith, Dan, and Chris, October 2006

affiliation with our family business, The Wandering Bull, have served to encourage and enrich this passion. When asked to share some memories, he offered thoughts on both Powwows and people who had made a significant impression on him and we shall share some of them with you so that you can get a different (younger) perspective. It can be interesting to see things through your child's eyes.

Andy's favorite Powwows were the ones in the early 1970's at Lafayette, Rhode Island, sponsored by the American Indian Federation, as well as the one sponsored by the Blackstone Valley Historical Society at Limerock, Rhode Island, and those put on by the North American Indian Club in Connecticut. They were exciting to him as a child, and perhaps he was not aware of the planning and work involved. The music depended upon who showed up with a drum. Often the make-shift drum arrived at midnight and started a "49"Session – the whole camp came alive and hurried out to see what the excitement was. Dancing was in a cornfield, up a hill, or on dust - Andy really enjoyed the spontaneity of those groups.

There were only three or four Powwows in a summer –so each one was such a special time. There are so many Powwows each summer now that there is less urgency to attend - there will always be another one very soon.

Of "modern day" Powwows, Andy's favorite was the one which had been held each year in York Beach, Maine. Having our whole family participate was most special and Ed and crew managed to rekindle the spirit and spontaneity of the "old" Powwows. He enjoyed seeing so many people unite to truly Powwow. Perhaps, he would now add the Mt. Kearsarge Indian Museum Powwow to his list of favorite modern day Powwows as well.

As a child, Andy was intimidated by Princess Necia mainly because she tended to be abrupt in word and action. At that time he could not see her purpose but later realized that she always had a purpose. It took Andy years to understand and appreciate the work both Princess Necia and her husband Chief Broken Arrow did on behalf of the Native people. She had a unique way of accomplishing things, which Andy came to admire - she had passion and determination.

Much of Andy's introduction to Powwows was guided by Princess Nashaweena. In his words, "She was the first 'old lady' I knew who was tough as nails on the outside and gentle on the inside." He saw how she was able to persuade people to see things her way. Gentle persuasion is an art which will stand you in good stead for a lifetime and Andy was learning this at a young age. He told of how she spoke of buying and selling houses at a profit and was really surprised to hear a woman speak this way. A sharp businessperson, Princess Nashaweena felt that it was correct and proper to be compensated for your labors. Her familiar comment was, "If you do a job for nothing that is what you are worth - nothing."

Princess Winona had a huge role in encouraging Andy's craftwork. Her Friday night bead classes were legendary and much was learned during those sessions. This bead class was the highlight of his week and the impetus for a lifelong love of beading and craftwork. Bead class was an opportunity to spend time with people he admired and looked up to. Andy has many fond memories of Princess Winona, but one stands out. When his classes at Trent University were completed for the school year, he and a fellow student decided to ride their bikes from Ontario home to Attleboro, Massachusetts. They had many adventures along the way, but none as special as the night they completed their sixth travel day. It was 11:30 pm and the two youngsters found themselves close to Worcester, Massachusetts and Winona's home. Andy called this 70 year old woman who quickly said, "Come right over and spend the night here." When they arrived around 2:00 am she had a big hug, a warm welcome, a comfortable bed, and food for the weary travelers.

To Andy, Star and Clear Sky were the most regal Native couple he has ever known. They exemplified tradition and class. Andy spent some time with them following his high school graduation, learning silversmithing and about their traditions and culture.

From Lou and Louise Deer, Andy learned about the Mohawk traditions and heard many stories about the iron work that Lou did on the high rise buildings in Manhattan and on the bridges in the area. It was very dangerous work and some of the stories were frightening. They were a fun loving couple –laughter and teasing were always the order of the day.

At the American Indian Federation Powwow, Andy learned all of the tasks necessary to ensure a smooth running event. He helped in every aspect and learned where the tipi poles were kept, how the rope was put up to outline the dance area, how to set up the speakers, how to keep the soda cold for the two day celebration, and a myriad of other things.

One Feather (Chris) found it hard to determine one favorite Powwow. He remembers the American Indian Federation Powwow as being very important because as a young child, it was the first one in which he really had an active part. He recalls getting the ice and helping Big Thunder (Fred Reynolds) cool the soda – this was a time consuming process and he was part of it. Moving ahead in time he notes that the American Indianist Society (AIS) May Dance became important to him because he worked hard to increase the quality of the event and assist the group to move forward. Today, the Mt. Kearsarge Indian Museum (MKIM) Powwow stands out as being a very welcoming event with excellent music and many great dancers.

One of the advantages for Chris, of knowing so many of the "old time people" was being able to look up to these adults for guidance and information. Certainly Princess Winona excelled at craftwork and was most willing to teach and to share her expertise. Star and Clear Sky taught him about the Southwest – the dances and music, the outfits and the culture. When they performed, the main purpose was to educate the spectators and at the same time, they were educating us as well.

One Feather (Chris) remembers Friday night bead class as well. He remembers our VW Bus being filled with kids and anyone else who wanted to come along on the ride to

Worcester. Sam One Bull (Paul Fadden) had a trading post at that time and would bring beads to sell. At 65 cents a hank, they were a real bargain. Unfortunately, the price of beads has risen since those days!

Chris' real love is Native American antiques. He finds it thrilling to own something that has been seen in a book or museum catalog. He also enjoys making reproductions, which involves research and study to get the colors and the technique correct – it is a challenge.

As the current owner with his wife Carolyn, Chris is proud to carry on the Wandering Bull message. He feels that "the Bull" was the backbone of the things which they did growing up and as young adults. Under their direction, the business is thriving and they love working in an area which they cherish and which has enriched their lives. He is living his childhood dream every day.

Brown Bear (Dan) was more involved in the Native culture before he married and his family increased with four lively children. His craft and dance skills have been put on the back burner for the time being. He talked about our trip to Northern Quebec to dance at the Montagnais reserve on Lac Saint Jean. Dan's smattering of high school French got us by with the First Nations people who did not speak English. The events of the week included many games and displays of skill and strength, such as "Portage" in which men would hoist sand bags onto their backs to see who could go the furthest carrying this heavy load, and huge feasts featuring a variety of wild game cooked right on the main street in a fire pit. He remembers being treated extremely well, almost like "royalty." This was a memorable trip for all of us.

Dan remembers with fondness the Lafayette Powwows and

meetings. He was fascinated by the secret ballot process, with its black and white balls. He remembers preparing for the Powwow – cutting the grass and cleaning up the yard, painting the flag pole etc. On Powwow day it was all excitement. He remembers being able to help the "soda guy" and having the responsibility of going down to the basement and bringing up soda to prepare for the thirsty spectators. To Dan, Lafayette was a lot of fun. It was an interesting time to be part of something that big and when his Dad was made chief – that was - wow!

Dan recalls Princess Nashaweena as being always very nice but as an imposing figure. He remembers that she ruled with an iron fist but was one of the most generous people - she gave the kids several items which meant something to her and therefore a lot to them. It was a good feeling.

Eyes That Shine (Ed) had mixed thoughts about Powwows. As a kid he remembers preparing for the Powwow at Lafayette, the North American Indian Powwow, Limerock and of course Pointe Bleue. Ed feels that growing up in the Powwow scene, you see Powwows from all of your different ages and perspectives. As a kid, the Powwow experience was all about how it affected you and as you grow up, your perspective becomes larger – how this affects the community.

Bright Canoe did all of the singing, accompanied himself with a hand drum, and was also the Master of Ceremonies. That was a formidable task for one person. Today we try to have several drums and a Master of Ceremonies.

To Ed, Star and Clear Sky were just about the greatest overall influence. He thinks that Star and Clear Sky, with War Arrow (Steve Sando) and Esther Clear Sky, gave us the basis of our school programs because they always emphasized the educational aspect of Powwows. They tried to give the spectator a clearer picture of Native culture.

Ed talks about the people as being the most important part of the culture, because without the people, you have no culture. Ed wants to know about the people, the human part of the picture, whether it is pretty or not. Passing on a song or a story is of great importance to Ed. He treasures the song which Chief Marie gifted to him because of the human aspect of the gifting.

The people he has met through this great adventure of ours have greatly affected Ed. They have made him a better listener, a better family member, and a better father because he wants to give his children a foundation in humanity. This interest and focus started when he was younger and continues to the present.

He looks at a beaded bandoleer bag and wants to know about the person who beaded it, at a basket and wonders about the basket maker. Where did the designs come from? Did they see the flowers while picking rice? What is daily life like? "Joe Star was just a regular person - he delivered mail - he was just a guy. Why was his hoop dance better than anyone else's? If you can imagine him out on the plaza at Jemez, in the dust learning from his father, that puts the romance in there. Maybe romance is not the right word, and provenance may not be the right word, but it is just the authenticity."

Friday night bead class was also one of Ed's fond memories - as was stopping at Harry's Restaurant on Route 9 on the way home for a late night snack.

He remembers his love of dancing - all he wanted to do was dance. He asks, "Where else can men go out together and dance together and sing together and the athletes are the dancers and all this time is spent preparing for that fun family time?"

Popshela (Faith) was also named by Princess Nashaweena. This name, which means "Wild Flower," seemed to be very appropriate for our vibrant, lively young one. Popshela (Faith), being the youngest member of the family, has an interesting perspective on things.

She talks about Pointe Bleue as an amazing life experience. Staying in the dormitory of the residential school on the reserve made her wonder what it would be like to live in a boarding school while her parents were out in the bush trapping. She was surprised that the children her age knew very little about their own culture. She was learning about her own culture but they did not seem to be. She further stated that there was an understanding, a communication between the children and her. They found a way to communicate without having a shared language. She remembers the kindness and generosity she was shown by these youngsters.

Faith's memories of Star and Clear Sky are positive and heart-warming. They were kind and gentle, loving and non-judgmental. As a child she remembers seeing the love in their eyes for each other - respect and compassion. Star and Clear Sky always included us in their shows and performances. We spent a lot of time with their entire family.

Lou and Louise Deer were Faith's friends first - that may be because she made friends where ever she went. She then introduced them to us and a fast friendship was formed. She remembers Louie as being tall and stern, funny and mysterious - she took an immediate liking to him.

She also commented on Friday night bead class. From Faith's perspective it was a long ride and a late night. She recalls the adults chatting endlessly - it must have seemed that way for a small child.

She has always enjoyed a wide variety of crafts and continues even to the present. The same feeling is true of music. The Native drum, and Native music to this day wake her up and make her feel whole - complete and revitalized. It is what is in her heart.

Paul doing a school program in Worcester, MA, 1996 - Note grandson Jake Ginga on the right

It is clear that the Native Culture has had a profound effect on each of the six - each in a unique and different way just as they are unique and different adults. We always felt that the culture had a positive influence on them as they were growing up. The people they met, the values they learned, and the varied experiences all helped to mold them into caring, loving and thoughtful people. For that we shall always be grateful.

REMEMBERING

In writing a book such as this, there is always the danger of omitting someone who should certainly be included. There are so many good and kind people whose paths we have crossed and whose influence has had a profound effect on me and on my family. I mention a number of them now not in any specific order, certainly not in order of importance or of closeness - but with the desire to remember and to honor. We do not include contemporaries as that list would be endless.

Leading Canoe, (Charles Wells) was a kind and gentle man who lived in Attleboro, Massachusetts - actually not too far from our home. It was he who first invited me to attend the American Indian Federation Powwow in Lafayette Rhode Island. Although I had been interested in the Native Culture for many years this was my family's introduction to it.

Chief Bright Canoe in all his finery

Bright Canoe (Johnny Diabo) and his wife Minnie came from Brooklyn, New York to attend the Lafayette Powwow. Johnny was the Master of Ceremonies and provided the music for the dancing. Minnie ran their booth. For years we traveled with Johnny to do programs and Powwows all around New England, the New York/New Jersey/Pennsylvania area and into Canada. John and Minnie had two daughters who traveled with them as they were growing up. Both were lovely dancers and much in demand at Powwows.

Ben Massey and his wife

Emma were always at the Lafayette Powwow and generally attended most of the programs that Johnny Diabo planned. Ben was Navajo and always said that his Indian name was impossible for anyone to pronounce so he was known as Ben. Ben filled in for Johnny when a break was needed - he sang his own style and accompanied himself on a single hand drum. Emma and her sister ran the food concession at Lafayette Powwow - a difficult task for two people to handle.

Twin Skies (Louie Deer) and his wife Green Leaf (Louise Deer) were staunch supporters of any project on which Johnny Diabo was working. They all hailed from Caughnawaga Reserve outside Montreal, Canada and at that time were living in Brooklyn, New York. Lou and Louise became close and dear friends of our family and we spent many pleasant hours with them. Their two daughters traveled with them as they were growing up, but as adults both of them moved back to the Reserve and are still living there with their families. They have both settled into Reserve life far away from Brooklyn, New York.

Ben Massey, Princess Nashaweena, Louie Deer, and Paul, circa 1974

The Tomah family, especially Maxine, was very active in the North American Indian Club. Each member of this family was involved in making this a vibrant Native American intertribal group which was family oriented. They welcomed us into this group and were supportive as we found our way.

Kay Garland and family, particularly son, Tom, were always there, always working and helping things to run smoothly. They were active in the North American Indian Club and later ran Powwows on their own land.

Big Thunder (Fred Reynolds) lived in Plainville and was active in the American Indian Federation. He later formed an intertribal group here in the Attleboro area. The first Powwow of this group Wollomonuppoag Indian Council was held at the American Legion Hall on route 1A in Plainville, Massachusetts. We even got involved in cutting the grass at this location so that the dance arbor would be properly prepared. I am a charter member of this group, which now presents a Powwow on the grounds of La Salette Shrine in Attleboro each June.

Chief One Bear

One Bear (Raymond Tremblay) and his wife, Little Fawn (Margaret Tremblay) organized and founded TOPIC (The Order to Preserve Indian Culture), an intertribal group based in the Weymouth, Massachusetts area. They were friendly with Princess Necia and Chief George Broken Arrow both on and off the Powwow circuit. This group sponsors one Powwow annually and has regular meetings and socials. Since One Bear passed his grandson Craig Tremblay has guided the group in the footsteps of One Bear. This group meets at the Prouse Farm in Canton – a true union of the Native and conservation.

Sleeping Wolf (Paul Norbeck) and his wife Caroline often participated in the American Indian Federation Powwow. Sleepy's amazing gift with the English language frequently got him into interesting situations from which he could extricate himself with great ease. Not sure that I have ever had the pleasure of knowing anyone with such linguistic talent either before or since. His chosen profession as an educator must have made for some unusual classroom situations.

Red Deer (Billy Muniz) and his wife Barbara were very much on the scene in the 1970's and 80's. They often traveled with Joe Star and Clear Sky. I remember them being at the Topsfield Fair Powwows run by Star and Clear Sky very early on. Red Deer was an Apache but at that time lived in East Providence, Rhode Island. One of his "specialties" was pulling out a camera while in the dance circle and mimicking the spectators by appearing to take their pictures. That was a great hit with the audience.

Princess Nashaweena (Sadie Barrie) was the Squaw Sachem and a driving force in the American Indian Federation activities, a cherished Elder and friend of the Bullock family. Although she had been more involved in her earlier days, by the time we met her she pretty much limited herself to the activities of the Federation, seldom attending the functions of other groups. Early on in our friendship she named me and five of our children. Her personal life was separate from her Federation activities. She shared her home with her husband John and his brother Jim. Her devoted niece Mildred was very close to her.

Running Deer (John Brin) lived in Attleboro, Massachusetts for a number of years. He became very active in Wollomonuppoag, later becoming the chief of that group. He had an ongoing interest in the spiritual aspects of this culture and inspired the formation of the Medicine Society. Prior to his crossing over he enjoyed the solitude of his land in Vermont which he shared with family and friends. His wife Robin's Wing (Evelyn) continues to be active in this group.

Paul and Chief White Wolf at the York Beach Powwow

White Wolf (Lee Maddix) founded the Dighton Intertribal Indian Council. He was very much involved in protecting the Council Oak. This tree has had a significant place in the Native history of the Southeastern Massachusetts area. This group continues his work, running several Powwows annually, as well as socials and benefits. They also work to maintain the council hall which was obtained through the efforts of White Wolf. He left us too soon but his legacy lives on. His family continues to be active in the Native community.

Wild Cat (Paul Cloud-Caruolo) and Whippoorwill (Margaret Cloud-Caruolo) were an outstanding couple - both excellent dancers who participated in many Powwows. Wild Cat has crossed over but Whippoorwill continues to provide us with a role model and shares her wisdom and knowledge.

Spotted Eagle (Ken Brown) was a respected Elder in Providence, Rhode Island. He loved to dance, enjoyed socializing at Powwows and socials, and freely shared his heritage. Often he would dance at a Powwow - truly enjoying the spirit of the circle and totally unaware of photographers who may have been sent to cover the event for their newspaper. It seemed as if without exception when the newspaper was published, Spotted Eagle's picture was front and center for all to see.

Supreme Medicine Man
Slow Turtle

Slow Turtle (John Peters) was Supreme Medicine Man of the Mashpee Wampanoag Tribe and a respected Elder. He and his wife Burne Stanley Peters have been very active in tribal affairs and Native issues. Slow Turtle has passed but will be remembered for his concern for the Natives, his confident dealings with others, and his leadership. Burne continues with their two daughters to spark the Massachusetts Center for Native American Awareness. This group has helped many in a myriad of ways.

Chief Spotted Eagle

Smiling One praising the beauty of the day, circa 1970

The Ranco family of Maine has been active in this culture for many years. We have known both brothers, Fred and Nick. Nick lived in Boothbay Harbor, Maine and for many years we purchased sweet grass from him, which we shipped to Native businesses all over the country. He and his family harvested the grass from his own special areas along the Maine seacoast, dried it as necessary and then delivered it to his customers. Each delivery we had from Nick was an adventure - his story telling was legendary. Fred, when we knew him, lived in New Hampshire and spent a good amount of time carving. He had a line of hand carved and painted items which were very popular at Powwows. A trip up to the Kangamangus Highway in New Hampshire to purchase these items was always a treat. Fred's wife, Jackie, currently lives in the area and is selling his book "Muskrat Stew."

Smiling One is remembered for her lovely smile and pleasant personality. She usually traveled alone and attended many New England Powwows in the 1970's and 80's. Her journey from New York via public transportation never seemed to tax her as she always had plenty of energy to dance her heart out.

Princess Red Wing was a well known figure in the New England area. Her tall, slender figure belied her strength and determination. She was a storyteller. Some of these stories were preserved on a series of tapes. These tapes were very popular in the 1980's and 90's but have since become unavailable.

Dick and Terry Naslund became involved in the Powwow world through their contact with our Boy Scout Dance Team. They traveled throughout New England attending Powwows and selling their sterling jewelry, Southwestern pottery and

Kachina Dolls. They journeyed to the Southwest annually to replenish their wares. Both passed away in 2011.

Black Eagle (Louie Ciarfella) was a dancer, craftsman, and all around good guy. He had a prominent place on the local Rex Trailer Show on television. Many children grew up watching this show in the Boston, Massachusetts area. His vocation as a chef paled to his avocation as a craftsman and creator of all things Indian. He has joined the Creator, but leaves his family who are following in his footsteps. His influence is still being felt through them.

Paul leading Don Brennan, Little Bear,
and Paul Levasseur

AFTERWORD

Written by Harriett Bullock

Our life together has been an amazing and wonderful journey. Our family has had unique adventures and we are honored to have shared some of them on the pages of this book. In this book, so long in the writing, we have hoped to give you an understanding of the importance of Native Culture and Powwows. We have been fortunate to have shared our journey with so many wonderful people.

Whirling Thunder's earthly journey was complete on February 18, 2014. We wanted his final services to reflect the life he lived. It was humbling to see all of the people from many walks of life, who came to pay their respects to this man who had meant so much to so many. All were in awe when on that snowy Friday evening in February the Creator sent us a thunder and lightning storm. Was this sent as a tribute to Whirling Thunder? We are deeply indebted to each and every person who honored Paul – by their presence, their words, their songs, and their music. The Traveling Song and the MicMac Honor Song, both so beautifully sung, surely reached the Heavens. This was certainly a learning experience for us all. Whirling Thunder had devoted his life to educating people about Native Cultures. In some small way, we hope to continue this journey that he started here on earth. He remains a vital and strong part of our lives – his legacy lives on through our children, grandchildren and great grandchildren.

We would like to leave you with this blessing which was so dear to him.

MAY YOUR OWN PERSONAL GREAT SPIRIT
WRITE HAPPINESS IN YOUR HEART

AND MAY THE RAINBOW ALWAYS TOUCH
UPON YOUR SHOULDER.

Winona - 41, 78, 121f

Orgs. 42

Powwows 57 f

"Sachem" 61-3

Tall Oak 80

Wildcat 86

Nr Fisher 89

? Nampashamet

Pr Necia 126, 138f, picture 142 - there is a resemblance to me!

Big ~~Toe~~ 126

Slow Turtle 126

CPSIA information can be obtained at www.ICGtesting.com
Printed in the USA
BVOW05s0332230915

419159BV00005B/41/P